Contents

An Angler's Guide to

AQUATIC INSECTS
AND
THEIR IMITATIONS

Rick Hafele and Scott Roederer
Illustrations by Richard Bunse

Johnson Books: Boulder

Spring Creek Press: Estes Park

Cover design: Kathleen Paoli

First Edition
1 2 3 4 5 6 7 8 9

ISBN 1-55566-003-7
LCCCN 86-82975

Printed in the United States of America by
Johnson Publishing Company
1880 South 57th Court
Boulder, Colorado 80301

Foreword

Most books written about aquatic insects have been written by flyfishers who were not entomologists or by entomologists who were not flyfishers. One of the authors of this one is an aquatic entomologist, and both he and his co-author are devout flyfishers.

Also, most books on aquatic entomology by entomologists were for use by teachers as textbooks and were largely methods of procedure for identification, with little or none of the behavioral information that the flyfisher needs.

All of the information in this one is presented with *only* the flyfisher in mind, thus all of it is useful to the flyfisher. Both the nymph fisher and the dry-fly fisher will find here what is needed to help them deal with their particular problems in identification and use of the artificial of choice.

The organization of the book is simple and easily followed, and always the purpose is to lead the reader to the proper use of the correct fly. The keys are arranged for the flyfisher's use and not for the student of entomology. There is no extraneous material.

There *is* much incidental material reflecting the authors' great interest in flyfishing and the application of their experiences. All of it is relevant. Simply absorbing this in the course of reading the book will make the reader a better rounded flyfisher.

The feeding *needs* of fish are presented, along with the reasons why those needs have become ingrained into habits over millions of years. Thus, you will learn why a fish feeds randomly at times and selectively at times, and you will learn which course to pursue in its time.

One does not have to be an "expert" flyfisher to use or learn from this book. In fact, the less expert the reader, the more will be learned, and all the information will be useful to the flyfisher.

The information in Chapter 10 on the caddis—probably the most important of all aquatic insects to the flyfisher—is the best and most complete of *any* book I've seen, and every bit of that information is useful to the flyfisher. This one chapter alone is worth the price of the book.

An Angler's Guide to Aquatic Insects and Their Imitations is a field guide, to be taken along in pocket or vest just like the rest of one's gear for flyfishing. Memory is a great tool, if you have it. Having the book along is a better tool.

I have a large leather book with a dozen or so clear plastic envelopes for carrying wet flies and nymphs. It will hold two or three hundred flies, all of which can be seen instantly by opening the book and turning the "pages." It makes finding and selecting the proper fly very quick and easy. It's called "Common Sense Fly Book."

That's a pretty good description of this one.

Charles E. Brooks
West Yellowstone, Montana

Introduction

"What's the use of their having names," the Gnat said, "if they won't answer to them?"

"No use to *them," said Alice, "but it's useful to the people that name them, I suppose."*

Lewis Carroll

It's true that Blue-Winged Olives will never answer to their name. It is, however, useful for us flyfishermen to have a name for them. For one thing, it allows us to communicate about hatches and fly patterns without saying something like: "You know, that little bug with the kind of olive body and the long tails and grayish-blue wings that stand straight up."

Being able to communicate about insects, using either the common names given them by flyfishermen or the scientific names given them by entomologists, has proven very useful indeed. It has allowed us to organize and study the insects and their life cycles, and that knowledge is beginning to be used extensively by flyfishermen to increase their understanding of how, when, and why fish feed. That understanding is, in turn, adding a new appreciation to the sport for those anglers, and it's increasing their success rate.

Flyfishermen spend hours tying flies that will prove slightly more effective or useful. They purchase equipment they think will be the most useful. They practice casting techniques, so the fly can be presented in the most useful manner. With usefulness being of such great importance to them and the study of insects being so useful, we're continually surprised how many flyfishermen, even very experienced ones, shy away from the study of aquatic insects.

Beginners are often too busy learning about fly patterns and flyfishing techniques to have much time left to think about aquatic insects, and many anglers, beginners and experts alike, feel the study of aquatic insects is too complicated and too scientific. All the Latin names, hatch charts, and anatomical terms sound too much like a high school or college biology class.

Spending the time to learn how to identify insects and learn about their behavior just doesn't seem useful— at first! But sooner or later there comes a day when fish are feeding heavily, and none of your flies work. What are the fish taking? How are they feeding? What should you use? The usefulness of knowing about aquatic insects becomes frustratingly apparent.

Three problems typically face the flyfisher-turned-entomologist at this point, and we've tried to solve each in this Waterwise Guide. Here are the problems:

Where to begin learning about aquatic insects. Many flyfishing books have been written that discuss, in depth, specific insect groups. Mayflies, stoneflies, and caddisflies have been the subjects of full-length books published in the last 10 years. By their design these books assume the reader already has some knowledge of entomology and that he can tell the difference, for instance, between a mayfly and a caddisfly. The result is that people without that basic knowledge become frustrated, misinterpret the information, and too often conclude that it's not useful to "know your bugs."

This guide book is designed for anglers with no prior knowledge of aquatic insects, as well as for those who can recognize aquatic insects but feel they need additional help in identifying them and understanding their behavior. Because it starts with the basics, we feel it's a great book (naturally) to begin learning about aquatic insects. And because it can be used for fairly complicated identifications, those who have been fishing for decades can also profit from this book.

How much information is necessary. Some books discuss in great detail dozens of specific species. It's not practical nor necessary for the angler to devote the time needed to learn about all of the thousands of species of aquatic insects. A simpler approach is more useful and certainly less disconcerting.

This book provides the basic information that's necessary and provides it in a simplified form. The keys identify insects into groups that are the most useful for anglers. Grouping the insects in this way provides truly practical information without going into such detail that you'll become lost and confused. This won't be the only entomology text you'll ever need or want, but it's an excellent starting point. After you learn to use this guide effectively, other, more detailed books will become understandable and useful.

How to use a knowledge of aquatic insects to improve fishing success. In the study of aquatic insects, this is the final and most important step for the angler. When you can go to a stream or lake, recognize the insects fish are feeding on, know how the insects live in the water, and select the pattern and tactic to match the natural, you'll

discover the greatest usefulness of understanding aquatic insects—
you'll catch more fish! No other sport depends so heavily on an
understanding of nature for its success.

This guide provides information on how to use a knowledge of
aquatic insects to improve your fishing. All the information presented in this guide will be applied to fishing. In addition to identifying insects and learning their way of life, you'll be given patterns
and tactics to use in imitating them successfully.

Organization

This Waterwise Guide covers the nine orders of insects that
contain important aquatic species. An understanding of these aquatic groups will provide the information needed for successful fishing
in most situations. The guide does not cover terrestrial insects that
may fall into the water, aquatic crustaceans, leeches, or baitfish.
These groups can be important food for fish and are necessary to
imitate at certain times. Including these groups, however, would
needlessly complicate the guide and reduce its usefulness.

The first four chapters provide the groundwork for using the
rest of the guide effectively. Chapter 1 discusses insect anatomy,
life cycles, and collecting techniques. This information is referred
to often throughout the text. Chapters 2 and 3 discuss fly pattern
selection and fishing strategies. This is where you'll learn how to
put to use the information presented in the remaining chapters.
Chapter 4 provides the first steps in identifying aquatic insects. It
will tell you the life stage and order of aquatic insect you have
collected, then tell where to proceed in the guide for more detailed
information.

Each of the remaining chapters discusses one of the nine orders
of insects covered by the guide. Information in each chapter covers
identification tips and keys, size range of the insects, life cycle,
North American distribution, habitat preferences and behavior,
emergence periods, and a summary of patterns and tactics.

To use the information provided in these chapters, you'll need
to become familiar with several abbreviations. In the charts on
major hatches, average sizes of each life stage of the insects are
given. The life stages are abbreviated as follows: N = nymph; A
= adult; P = pupa. Those charts also indicate the distribution
of the insects in North America as follows: E = eastern section;
C = central section; W = western section.

In the charts on major patterns and tactics, the column headed

"Ref." gives references where the fly pattern can be found. The numbers indicate books listed on page 28. The tactics column gives the numbers of appropriate flyfishing tactics as described on pages 32-40.

How to Use the Keys

The identification keys are a major part of each chapter. Many people unfamiliar with keys feel threatened by them. Don't let them intimidate you. With practice they'll become quick "road maps" to the underwater life of streams and lakes. It does require practice to use them, however, and we urge you not to become discouraged in your first attempts at identification. Remember your first attempts at fly casting?

The keys in this guide are designed for simplicity and accuracy. Here's how to use them:

The keys used are called dichotomous keys. This means they are made up of a series of couplets. Each couplet presents two different descriptions or lists of characteristics. After reading each description, choose the one that *best* matches the insect you're trying to identify.

Pay close attention to the wording in each couplet. For example, the statement, "One pair of wings and long tails present," means your insect *must* have both one pair of wings and long tails. Another description may read "Two or three tails present." This means your insect must have tails, but either two or three tails may be present. (Always check carefully to be sure that fragile features like tails weren't broken off when you collected or preserved your specimen.)

Each description is followed by a number or by the name of an insect group. If a number is given, it tells you which couplet to go to next. Proceed to that couplet and again compare your insect to the two descriptions. If there is a name after the couplet that best describes your insect, it is the name of the insect you have collected or of its group. Following the name will be a page number telling you where to turn for a more specific key or for additional information about the insect.

Until you become familiar with aquatic insects, begin each identification process with the Key to Life Stages, p. 44. It will help you determine which life stage the insect is in and will direct you to the next key. That key will, in turn, help you identify the insect to its order and will direct you to the appropriate chapter.

Always start at the beginning of each key as you proceed. If neither description in a couplet seems to match the insect, return to the last couplet you considered to see if you made an error. For accuracy there is an illustration of the major characteristics described in each couplet. Compare these illustrations with your insect.

For simplicity, the keys try to describe characteristics that are easily seen and understood, but for accuracy, it is sometimes essential to use features that are small or difficult to see. A small hand lens or loupe will help you see them more clearly. The use of some kind of magnifier is necessary if you wish to complete all the identifications possible with this guide. Magnifying aids are available from some of our flyfishing shops and catalogs or from the biological supply houses listed at the end of Chapter 1. You may also find a suitable lens at your local drugstore in the section on reading aids or at your local photo store where loupes and magnifiers are sold as aids in viewing slides.

This book is a "field guide". Keep it in a pocket or your fishing vest or bag. Start looking for and collecting insects each time you fish. *An Angler's Guide to Aquatic Insects and Their Imitations* will help you determine what they are, their importance, and how to imitate them. Don't be surprised if suddenly your fishing becomes more interesting, more productive, and more satisfying. That's our intent.

Rick Hafele
Scott Roederer

1. "Bugs Is Not a Four-Letter Word

The first steps in the identification and study of aquatic insects are the most difficult, as they are with any new skill or subject. In addition, studying insects presents several unique problems. First, their small size and secretive habits require special techniques and careful observation just to find them. Second, their shape and structure are highly variable and quite different from those of other animals we're used to seeing. As a result, many terms used to describe the anatomy and general biology of insects are unfamiliar and must be learned. And third, their astounding diversity often overwhelms beginners, stopping them before they get past the first few hurdles.

The goal of this chapter is to provide you with the groundwork for making those first steps and meeting the special challenges of studying insects. Once you get on your way, an incredible world will open up, one that holds many secrets to angling success.

What's a bug?

Perhaps the first question to ask is: What is an insect? To answer it we must first look at how animals are classified. Zoologists have created a hierarchical system that all animals can be placed in. The basic categories of this hierarchy are listed below:

Kingdom
  Phylum
    Class
      Order
        Family
          Genus
            Species

The top category, kingdom, is the broadest and most general. Each successive category more closely defines the animal in question. "Species" is the most specific category. A species is a group of individuals or populations that in nature interbreed and produce fertile offspring. When a species is listed, the genus and species name are always listed together in italics with the genus name capitalized. For example, *Ephemerella subvaria* is a species of mayfly, commonly called the Hendrickson.

The relationship of animals within each category is based on evolutionary connections and morphological and physiological similarities. Remember, this is a scheme developed by biologists to help classify the thousands of animals found in the world. Not all animals fit neatly into this scheme, and some are reclassified as more is learned about their morphology and biology. This can be frustrating for amateur naturalists who find the scientific name of a familiar animal has been changed.

Using the above categories, an insect (a Golden Stonefly in our example) would be classified as follows:

Kingdom = Animal.

Phylum = Arthropoda. This phylum includes all animals with an exoskeleton and jointed legs. Besides insects, it includes crustaceans (e.g. crabs, crayfish, shrimp, and sowbugs), centipedes, millipedes, spiders, and mites.

Class = Insecta. This is the division that separates insects from other arthropods. The basic characteristics of all adult insects are:
— One pair of antennae.
— Three distinct body regions: head, thorax, abdomen.
— Three pairs of jointed legs on the thorax.
— No jointed legs on the abdomen.
— Often one or two pairs of wings on the thorax.

Order = Plecoptera (stoneflies, e.g.). This division divides the insects into major groups. Mayflies, stoneflies, and caddisflies, for instance, are all "orders" of insects.

Family, Genus, and **Species** = Perlidae: *Acroneuria californica* (Golden Stonefly, e.g.). These divisions further define specific types of insects.

Life Stages of Insects

Identifying insects is further complicated because of the different stages they pass through during their development. The changes that occur from the egg stage to the adult are often dramatic. The incredible change of a caterpillar into a butterfly is well known. Most aquatic insects experience similar changes.

The process of changing form during the life cycle is called **metamorphosis**. Three types of metamorphosis are possible: ametabolous, incomplete, and complete.

Ametabolous Metamorphosis. This type of metamorphosis means without change and refers to the lack of change between the immature and adult stages. It's found only in a few very primitive orders of insects that have no wings as adults (e.g. Order Collembola). Some species are semiaquatic, but they're not important to anglers.

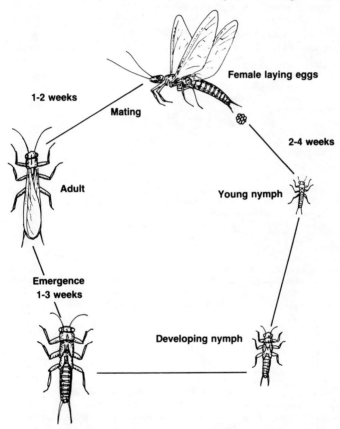

Female laying eggs

1-2 weeks

Mating

2-4 weeks

Adult

Young nymph

**Emergence
1-3 weeks**

Developing nymph

Incomplete Metamorphosis. Insects with incomplete metamorphosis pass through three distinct stages: egg, nymph, and adult. The time required to complete each stage varies widely. Normally the greatest amount of time is spent in the nymphal stage. In most cases, the entire cycle requires one year to complete, although this also varies with different species. (More specific information on life cycles is listed in the chapters on the different orders of insects.) Nymphs often look similar to their adult stage. As nymphs mature, the adult wings begin developing in stiff pouch-like structures on the thorax called **wing pads**. This is an obvious and unique characteristic of insects with incomplete metamorphosis. The wing pads on fully mature nymphs will be quite dark, almost black, in color. The orders of aquatic insects with incomplete metamorphosis include:

Mayflies (Order Ephemeroptera)
Dragonflies and Damselflies (Order Odonata)
Stoneflies (Order Plecoptera)
Water Bugs (Order Hemiptera)

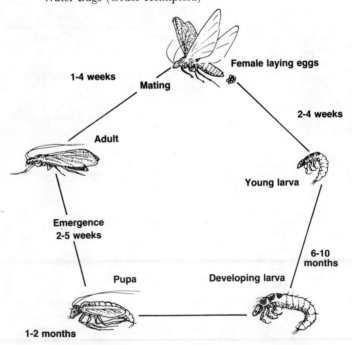

Complete Metamorphosis. Insects with complete metamorphosis pass through four distinct stages: egg, larva, pupa, and adult. The addition of the pupal stage separates insects with complete metamorphosis from those with incomplete metamorphosis. While the length of time needed to complete each stage again varies widely, the entire cycle usually takes one year. Most of the cycle is generally spent in the larval stage. Unlike nymphs, larvae bear little resemblance to the adults and show no development of wing pads. It is during the pupal stage that the wing pads and other adult features develop. The orders of aquatic insects with complete metamorphosis include:

> Dobsonflies and Alderflies (Order Megaloptera)
> Caddisflies (Order Trichoptera)
> Aquatic Moths (Order Lepidoptera)
> Aquatic Flies (Order Diptera)
> Aquatic Beetles (Order Coleoptera)

Growth and Development

The growth of insects occurs in a series of stages called **instars**. The exoskeletons of insects must be periodically shed in order for growth to continue. The process of shedding the old exoskeleton is called **molting**. When the old exoskeleton is cast aside, a new, slightly larger one is present underneath. The old empty exoskeleton is often referred to as a **shuck**. Except for mayflies, molting stops once the insect reaches the winged adult stage. Most insects molt five or six times during their development. Mayflies, stoneflies, dragonflies, and damselflies, however, may molt 15-30 times before reaching the adult stage.

Recognizing the insect's stage and degree of development can help the angler determine what insect to imitate. Mature nymphs and larvae often become more active in the water as they move to emergence or pupation sites. This increased activity makes them more available to fish and, thus, makes them more important to imitate. Looking for and imitating the most mature insects will normally produce the best fishing.

One of the most vulnerable periods in the insect's life cycle is during emergence from the immature to the adult stage. At the time of emergence, mature nymphs or pupae typically crawl out of the water or swim to the water's surface. Those that emerge in the surface film must break through the surface tension, and that can take from several seconds to over a minute. Thus, during emergence, the insects are no longer protected by the shelter of the lake or stream bottom. Fish readily take advantage of the insects' vulnerability and often feed selectively on emerging nymphs or pupae. The angler who recognizes this activity will find fast fishing by imitating the shape and action of the natural.

Adult insects often rest on the water's surface after emerging from the nymphal or pupal shuck. Then, after mating, most aquatic insects return to the water to lay their eggs. Insects resting or laying eggs on the surface provide fish with many easy meals. These are the times when fishing dry flies is most effective. Use a fly that matches the size, shape, and color of the natural, and fish it with the action of the natural.

Insect Anatomy

In order to use this field guide or any other guide to insects, a basic understanding of insect anatomy is essential. Insects have many unique shapes and structures. As a result, entomologists have developed specific terms to describe them. The illustration below shows the general structure of an insect.

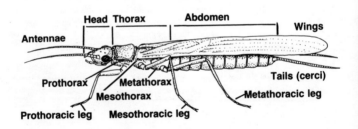

The body of an insect is divided into three major sections: head, thorax, and abdomen. Let's look at each of these sections in greater detail.

Head

The eyes, antennae, and mouth parts are the major structures of the head most frequently used in identification.

Eyes. Nymphal, pupal, and adult stages of most insects possess a pair of large compound eyes. Compound eyes are made up of many individual lenses called facets. Insect larvae lack compound eyes.

Instead, they have a cluster of small eye spots on each side of the head called **stemmata**.

Ocelli. In addition to compound eyes, many insects also possess two or three small eye spots near the center or top of the head called **ocelli**. The location and number of ocelli are often used to distinguish different insects.

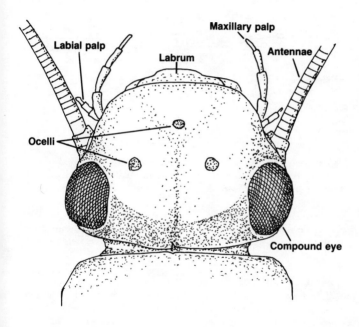

Antennae. Antennae are usually obvious features on insects. All adult insects have one pair. Their size, shape, and location on the head, however, vary widely.

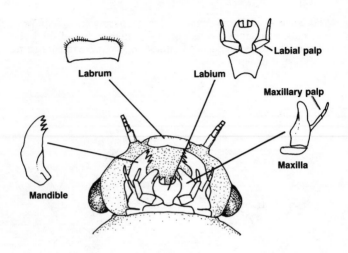

Mouth Parts. The mouth parts of all insects are composed of four distinct structures: **labrum** (upper lip), **mandibles**, **maxillae**, and **labium** (lower lip). The maxillae and labium often possess a pair of finger-like structures called maxillary palpi and labial palpi, respectively. Insects feed on many types of food in many different ways. To feed effectively, the four basic parts of the mouth have evolved into many different shapes. These variations help in identification.

Thorax

The most distinct features of the thorax are three pairs of jointed legs and usually one or two pairs of wings. Immature insects lack wings, although nymphs and pupae show the developing wings as wing pads. Insect larvae always lack wing pads and may even lack legs.

The thorax is divided into three sections: **prothorax** (first thoracic segment, closest to the head), **mesothorax** (second thoracic segment), and **metathorax** (third thoracic segment). The dorsal (top) surface of the thoracic segments are called **nota**, the sides **pleura**, and the ventral (bottom) surface **sterna.**

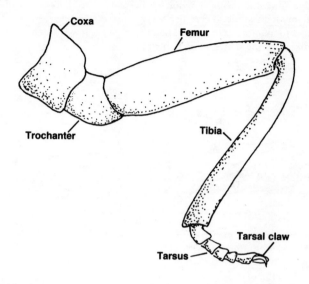

Legs. Insect legs come in various shapes and sizes, but they are all composed of six separate parts:

Coxa—The closest to the body or basal segment.

Trochanter—A small segment following the coxa.

Femur—The first long major segment of the leg.

Tibia—The second long segment of the leg.

Tarsus (pl. Tarsi)—A group of small segments usually one to five in number at the foot of the leg.

Tarsal Claw—One or two claw-like structures at the tip of the leg.

Wings. Wings are a major structure on most adult insects. The relative shape and size of the wings are often used to recognize different orders of insects. Wings are also important for identifying different adult insects within an order. For this, **wing venation** is typically used.

Wing venation refers to the pattern or placement of veins within the wing. All the major veins and most minor veins have been named. Deciphering wing venation can be tricky, but at times it is the most effective method of identifying adults. Because of possible difficulties, wing venation has been avoided wherever possible in this field guide. There are several places, however, where it's used to maintain accuracy. The illustration below is a generalized wing with the major veins named.

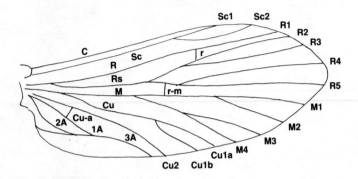

Major longitudinal veins (abbreviations in parentheses):
      Costa (C)
      Subcosta (Sc)
      Radius (R)
      Radial Sector (Rs)
      Media (M)
      Cubitus (Cu)
      Anal Veins (A)

Many longitudinal veins divide into several branches as they reach the tip of the wings. The different branches are designated as R1, R2, R3 or M1, M2, M3, etc.

Major cross veins (examples illustrated above):
      Humeral (h)
      Radial (r)
      Sectorial (s)
      Radio-medial (r-m)
      Medial (m)
      Medio-cubital (m-cu)
      Cubito-anal (cu-a)

Specific examples of wing venation are illustrated where referred to in the keys.

Abdomen

The abdomen consists of six to 11 segments. The eleventh segment is generally greatly reduced, and most insects appear to have 10 abdominal segments. The dorsal (top) surface of each segment is called the **terga**, and the ventral (bottom) surface is called the **sterna**.

The tip of the abdomen of adult insects contains the reproductive organs and occasionally two or three **cerci** (tails). Immature aquatic insects may also have various numbers and types of gills, lateral filaments, hooks, or simple unsegmented legs called **prolegs** on the abdomen. These structures are often useful in identification and are illustrated in the keys where necessary.

In using the guide, please note that the length of an insect does not include the tails or antennae unless specified. Length will usually indicate the distance from front of head to tip of abdomen.

Collecting Techniques

Collecting aquatic insects is normally quite simple. The major difficulty is setting aside the time to do it. Since collecting is often done during a fishing trip, taking the time to do it requires some self-discipline. Just a 10 minute break in the fishing will result in enough insects for an evening's study. Of course, if the fish are being selective and you collect some samples to try and match the hatch, you won't want to wait for the evening to identify them. Try carrying this guide with you on your next trip. It might save the day.

Observation is a key element of all collecting. Many people walk within inches of adult insects sitting on branches or leaves of trees and shrubs without ever seeing them. As you spend more time collecting and observing, you'll find that lakes and streams which once seemed relatively devoid of insect life are suddenly alive.

Let's first look at ways to collect the underwater stages of aquatic insects. The easiest way to start collecting is simply with your hands. Find a shallow riffle in a stream or a shoreline area in a lake and start picking up rocks, aquatic plants, or pieces of wood. Lift them slowly so the insects won't be washed off. It helps to have a small white tray (12"x8"x1", for example) in which to place the insects. The tray makes it easy to see the shape, color, and swimming behavior of the different insects. You may be able to locate a suitable tray at an art supplies store or through one of the entomological supply catalogs listed later in this chapter.

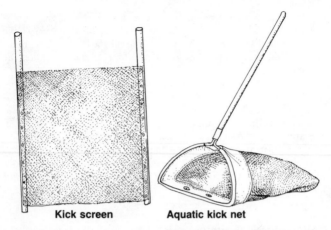

Kick screen   **Aquatic kick net**

A more efficient method for collecting in streams is to use a kick screen. A kick screen can be made by attaching a piece of window screen three square feet in size between two four-foot long, one-inch dowels. Facing downstream, hold the screen firmly on the stream bottom. Turn over rocks upstream of the screen with your feet (hence the term, "kick screen" or "kick net") until you have disturbed several square feet of stream bottom. The current will wash dislodged insects onto the screen. Carefully lift the screen out of the water and carry it to the bank. You can then sort the insects out of the debris and place them in the tray. Sample areas of different depths and velocities for a thorough picture of what insects are present and how abundant they are. You'll be amazed at the variety and numbers of insects collected.

For effective collecting in lakes, use an aquatic kick net. This is made of a heavy wire hoop 12-15 inches in diameter attached to a three- to five-foot wooden handle. A canvas bag with a fine mesh bottom is attached to the hoop. This net can be used in streams just like the kick screen, and in lakes it can be dragged along the bottom or through weed beds. Insects are washed into the back of the net bag and cannot easily swim out. These nets are available from BioQuip, which has a full line of collecting and preserving equipment (see listing of sources at the end of this section), or they can be homemade.

Collecting adults is best done with a standard butterfly net.

Sweep it over shoreline vegetation to find resting adults. A butterfly net will be a big help when adults are swarming over the water as well. If a net is not available, adults can be collected easily early in the morning just after sunrise. Look carefully on the shoreline foliage. The insects are usually too cold early in the morning to fly away, making them easy to pick up. Also shake the branches of trees along streams and lakes to see what adults fly out.

If all this sounds like a bit too much to begin with, simplify it. Stick an aquarium net in your vest pocket along with a zip-lock bag with the following items: a pair of tweezers, a few vials, and the white lid off a pickle jar. Along with this book and your curiosity, that's all you'll need. Of course, you'll soon find that a magnifying lens would make it easier and more fun. Then you'll want that bigger net and then . . .

You may be worried about being bitten while collecting or handling aquatic insects. Generally this isn't a problem. Only a few insects, particularly hellgrammites and some water bugs, are capable of biting. To avoid any problems, handle insects with forceps or tweezers or hold them loosely in an open hand. By handling them gently, even the fiercest larva will be more concerned about finding its way back to the water than it will be about feeding on your hand.

Preserve aquatic insects (immatures and adults) for later reference by putting them in glass vials filled with 80% ethyl alcohol. Isopropyl alcohol (rubbing alcohol) can also be used, but it will make insects more brittle than ethyl alcohol. Alcohol will change the color of insects over time. There are more complicated chemicals that can be used to prevent color changes. They don't completely eliminate color changes, however, and they're more difficult to find, more expensive, and more dangerous to use. Thus, alcohol is generally your best choice.

Always label the samples you keep. With a soft lead pencil, write the date, location, and name of specimen (if known) on a piece of heavy white paper cut small enough to fit inside the vial. Where and when samples were taken will be quickly forgotten if they are not properly labeled. When carefully maintained, your collection will provide hours of fascination and lots of useful information.

Finally, collecting must be done with the same regard for the environment as fishing. Keep only the insects you need for later reference; return the rest to the stream or the lake. Take only a few samples from any one area to minimize the overall impact on insect numbers. Some states require permits for collecting aquatic insects— check regulations before sampling. If collecting is done with care and common sense, the effect on the environment will be negligible, and your awareness and appreciation of aquatic life will provide tremendous satisfaction over the years.

Sources for Sampling and Collecting Equipment

BioQuip Products
P.O. Box 61
Santa Monica, CA 90406
(213) 322-6636

Carolina Biological Supply Company
2700 York Rd.
Burlington, North Carolina 27215
or
P.O. Box 7
Gladstone, OR 97027

VWR Scientific
P.O. Box 1004
Norwalk, CA 90650
or
P.O. Box 3551, Terminal Annex
Seattle, WA 98124
or
P.O. Box 1678
Salt Lake City, UT 84110

References

If you want additional general information about aquatic entomology, the following references will be a good place to start. Also listed here is Rick Hafele's first book, co-authored with Dave Hughes, which gives extensive information about western species of aquatic insects.

Hafele, Rick and Dave Hughes. *The Complete Book of Western Hatches*. Portland, Oregon: Frank Amato Publications, 1981.

Lehmkuhl, D.M. *How to Know the Aquatic Insects*. Dubuque, Iowa: W.C. Brown, 1979.

McCafferty, W. Patrick. *Aquatic Entomology*. Boston: Science Books International, 1981.

Merritt, R.W., and K.W. Cummins. *An Introduction to the Aquatic Insects of North America*. Dubuque, Iowa: Kendall/Hunt Publishing Co., 1984 (2nd ed.).

Pennak, Robert W. *Fresh-Water Invertebrates of the United States*. New York: John Wiley & Sons, Inc., 1978 (2nd ed.).

Torre-Bueno, J.R. *A Glossary of Entomology*. New York: New York Entomological Society, 1978.

2. Fly Patterns: Theory and Design

The primary goal of this guide is to help you identify the insects on which fish feed. However, once an insect is identified, the obvious question is, "What pattern should I use to imitate it?". This question is asked many times, and it can often be answered several ways.

Many books have been written that discuss fly patterns in great detail (see reference list at the end of this chapter), and it's not necessary to list patterns here. Instead, this chapter analyzes basic pattern selection and design. It's difficult, however, to discuss fly patterns without first considering some aspects of the feeding behavior of fish.

Feeding Behavior

Fish are primitive creatures, and trout and salmon (family Salmonidae) are some of the earliest fishes. Their evolutionary roots go back more than 100 million years. The primitive nature of fish is a fortunate fact for flyfishers; if fish had reached a higher level of intelligence, even our best efforts as anglers would easily be seen as fake. As it is, certain configurations of fur and feather fool fish often enough to make flyfishing an entertaining and exciting sport.

But what causes fish to select a certain type of food? Above everything else, fish must receive enough energy from their food to maintain their health and grow. Therefore, the fish's food must supply more energy than the fish expends in capturing it. This may not be the case for each individual food item taken, but it must be true over the long run or the fish will weaken and die. To receive enough energy and to make the most of their feeding opportunities, fish sometimes feed "randomly" and other times "selectively."

Random Feeding

Random feeding simply means fish will take any food that is available. This might be called the "salad bar" approach. Trout in streams are known to suck up all types of things drifting in the currents, including items that aren't food, such as small sticks, leaves, or seed cases. The non-food items (like your fly) are quickly spit back out, while all else is swallowed.

Fish feed randomly most of the time, which may explain the effectiveness of many general nymph patterns. The intensity of this feeding, however, may vary during the day depending upon changes in light, temperature, and other weather conditions and depending upon the availability of food. Because morning and evening are periods of greater insect activity, they are good times to find fish feeding randomly. A fly that has the general shape of many insects and looks alive in the water will probably produce best during times of random feeding. The fly must still be presented near the fish, however, since they may not move to take the fly if other food is closer.

Selective Feeding

Selective feeding refers to a situation where fish are eating only one type of food, even though other food may also be present. They are like a five-year-old child who eats all of one item on his plate before starting the next. At first this may seem less energy efficient, since some food that is just as available is ignored. But by focusing all their attention on one abundant food item their feeding actually becomes more efficient and, therefore, reduces the overall energy expended.

Selective feeding occurs when one item of food is very abundant and available. This normally happens when nymphs and pupae become active just prior to or during emergence or when adults are on the surface just after emergence or when laying their eggs. During a large "hatch," fish will often feed with seeming abandon and will take insects within a few feet of a fisherman. But the selectivity of their feeding can make them very difficult to catch. Nothing in flyfishing is more exciting than having fish feed all around you, and nothing is more frustrating than to have them ignore all your offerings.

No one knows for sure how fish can select one food item so accurately, but it may be the result of a "search image." A search image means the fish picks out one or more specific characteristics of the insect hatching and looks only for those traits. When those characteristics are seen, the fish strikes. Other food is not even seen, because it doesn't match the search image. Therefore, to be successful, your fly doesn't have to be an exact copy of the natural insect, but it must possess the characteristics of the fish's search image.

Important factors in the fish's search image may include size, silhouette, color, and/or action of the natural. For insects on the water's surface, the light pattern created on the surface itself may also be important. These factors should be carefully considered when selecting a pattern during a major hatch, once you have determined the type of insect the fish are feeding on and its life stage.

Fly Patterns

Once you begin collecting and identifying aquatic insects, you will be amazed at their numbers and diversity. At first you might think you need a different pattern for every type of insect you find. This is neither practical nor necessary. A simpler approach is to select certain pattern styles that effectively imitate the major groups and stages of aquatic insects, then tie those styles in different colors and sizes. Studying aquatic insects can actually reduce the number of patterns you carry, because you'll have a better understanding of which insects can be imitated by the same pattern.

No pattern exactly duplicates a natural insect in appearance, but some come closer than others. The levels or degrees of imitation can be broken into three categories: suggestive, impressionistic, and imitative. Imitative patterns come the closest in accurately representing a real insect. They are generally tied to imitate one specific type of insect and are used when fish are feeding selectively. Imitative patterns are rarely needed, however. Too often flyfishers blame their failure on the pattern, when it's actually presentation or the life stage of the insect being imitated that's in error. Suggestive and impressionistic patterns try to imitate the general shape, size, and color of an insect. They are usually superior to imitative patterns because they are easier to tie, have more action in the water, and can represent more than one insect.

Examples of different levels of imitation for a caddis pupa:

> Suggestive—Soft Hackle
> Impressionistic—LaFontaine's Sparkle Pupa
> Imitative—Quill-Wing Caddis Pupa

Fish feed on every stage of the insect's life cycle. As a result, you'll need patterns that imitate each stage. A minimum of three types of patterns will be needed: nymphs, emergers, and dry flies.

Nymphs. Nymph patterns imitate the underwater nymph or larval stage of aquatic insects. This stage provides the bulk of the fish's diet, and nymph patterns are consistent producers. You will not be able to see fish feeding on nymphs in most cases. Therefore, you must read the water carefully to find the fish.

Emergers. Emerger patterns imitate nymphs or pupae swimming to the surface or hanging in the surface film during emergence. These forms of the insect provide easy meals and are taken greedily when abundant. If the insect is taken near the surface, fish will often make a distinctive riseform known as a head-and-tail rise. The rise will leave a swirl on the surface, but no bubble. Other times, when fast-moving pupae, particularly caddis pupae, are rising to the surface, fish may completely leave the water as a result of following the insect quickly to the surface. In spite of all the artists' renditions, very seldom does a fish jump clear of the water to take an adult insect on the wing. When fish are "jumping," try a caddis pupa imitation.

Dry Flies. Dry flies imitate insects on the water's surface. These can be adult aquatic insects after emerging and when laying eggs or terrestrial insects that have fallen into the water. Rises to surface flies may be subtle or violent, depending on the behavior of the insect. In either case, a bubble is usually left on the surface where the insect (or your fly) was sucked into the fish's mouth.

Once you have determined which stage of the insect to imitate, you must select a pattern that matches the appropriate type or order of insect. There are several basic styles of patterns that can be used to imitate the major groups of insects in their various life stages. These styles are depicted on the following pages. Use these styles as guides. By tying them in different colors and sizes, they can effectively imitate most of the insects found in each order.

Nymph Patterns

Mayflies

Gold-Ribbed Hare's Ear

Nymph Patterns (cont.)

Mayflies

Pheasant Tail

Stoneflies

Montana Stone

Damselflies

Polly's Damsel

Wiggle Damsel

Dragonflies

Brown Dragon

Caddisflies

Cased Caddis

Nymph Patterns (cont.)

Caddisflies

Latex Caddis

Fur-Bodied Caddis

Diptera

Midge Larva

Emerger Patterns*

Mayflies

Suspended Nymph

Caddisflies

Soft Hackle Emerger

Emerger Patterns (cont.)*

Caddisflies

Caddis Pupa

Diptera

Standard Midge Pupa

Reverse Midge Pupa

---

*Damselfies, dragonflies, and stoneflies crawl out of the water to emerge. Therefore, emerger patterns are not needed for these groups.

Dry Fly Patterns

Mayflies

Catskill Patterns

Parachute Mayfly

Compara-Dun

Dry Fly Patterns (cont.)

Stoneflies

Downwing Stonefly

Damselflies

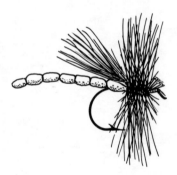

Adult Damsel

Caddisflies

Quill-Wing Caddis

Dry Fly Patterns (cont.)

Caddisflies

Elk Hair Caddis

Diptera

Standard Midge Adult

Griffith's Gnat

Fly Pattern Use Chart

The following chart lists a range of patterns for nymphs, emergers, and dry flies, and provides a quick reference for determining the water type and insect order for which they are best suited. There are, obviously, hundreds of patterns not listed, but these have proven effective in many locations and should provide a good starting point for pattern selection. Other patterns for specific insects are listed in the chapters discussing each insect order. Note that most patterns will imitate more than one insect if tied in varying sizes and colors. Explanations of the codes used is given beneath the chart.

Nymphs

Pattern	Water-Type Code					Insect Order Code				
	RF	RN	FL	PL	LK	MF	SF	DF	CF	DP
Hare's Ear	X	X	X	X	X	X	X		X	
Zug Bug	X	X	X			X			X	
Beaver Pelt	X	X				X	X			
Pheasant Tail	X	X	X	X	X	X	X			X
Box Canyon Stone	X	X				X				
Bird's Stone	X	X				X				
Fair Damsel			X	X	X			X		
PKCK Nymph			X	X	X					X

Emergers

Pattern	Water-Type Code					Insect Order Code				
	RF	RN	FL	PL	LK	MF	SF	DF	CF	DP
Soft Hackles	X	X	X		X	X	X		X	X
Flymphs	X	X	X	X	X	X	X		X	X
LaFontaine's Sparkle Pupa	X	X	X	X	X				X	
Carey Special			X		X			X	X	
Floating Nymph			X	X		X	X			

Dry Flies

Pattern	Water-Type Code					Insect Order Code				
	RF	RN	FL	PL	LK	MF	SF	DF	CF	DP
Wulff	X	X				X				
Humpy	X	X				X				
Compara-Dun			X	X	X	X				
Parachute Dun			X	X	X	X				
Compara-Spinner	X	X	X	X	X	X				
Sofa Pillow	X	X					X			
Blue Damsel			X	X	X			X		
Elk Hair Caddis	X	X	X	X	X				X	
Quill-Wing Caddis	X	X	X	X	X				X	
Midge Adults			X	X	X					X

Water-Type Codes:
RF—Riffle
RN—Run
FL—Flat
PL—Pool
LK—Lake

Insect Order Codes:
MF—Mayfly
SF—Stonefly
DF—Damselfly/Dragonfly
CF—Caddisfly
DP—Diptera

References

The following references have been numbered "1" through "11." **When a specific fly is mentioned in the coming chapters, these numbers are used to indicate the reference book that contains instructions on tying that pattern.** There are, of course, many other excellent references on fly patterns.

1. Bay, Kenneth E. *The American Fly Tyer's Handbook*. Tulsa, Oklahoma: Winchester Press, 1979.

2. Hughes, Dave. *American Fly Tying Manual*. Portland, Oregon: Frank Amato Publications, 1986.

3. Kaufmann, Randall. *American Nymph Fly Tying Manual*. Portland, Oregon: Salmon-Trout-Steelheader, 1975.

4. Leisenring, J., and V. Hidy. *The Art of Tying the Wet Fly and Fishing the Flymph*. New York: Crown, 1971.

5. Leonard, J. Edson. *Flies*. New York: A.S. Barnes and Co., 1950.

6. Roskelley, Fenton. *Flies of the Northwest*. Spokane, Washington: Inland Fly Fishing Club Publications, 1979.

7. Surette, Dick, ed. *Fly Tyer Pattern Bible*. North Conway, New Hampshire: Saco River Publishing Corp., 1985.

8. Helleckson, Terry. *Popular Fly Patterns*. Salt Lake City: Peregrine Smith, 1977.

9. Jorgensen, Poul. *Poul Jorgensen's Modern Trout Flies*. Garden City, New York: Doubleday, 1979.

10. Nemes, Sylvester. *The Soft-Hackled Fly Addict*. Old Greenwich, Connecticut: Chatham Press, 1975.

11. Rosborough, Polly. *Tying and Fishing the Fuzzy Nymphs*. Harrisburg, Pennsylvania: Stackpole, 1978.

3. Fishing Strategies

The effectiveness of a pattern is determined by two major factors: 1) how well it matches the size, shape, and color of the natural being imitated; and 2) how it is presented and retrieved. Chapter 2 discussed imitation and pattern selection. This chapter describes what to do after a pattern is tied on.

Just as pattern selection is based on the appearance of the natural, your tactics should be based on the behavior of the natural. Imitating behavior is as important as pattern selection, if not more important, and is unquestionably the more difficult to learn.

The appearance of an insect can be seen by simply collecting it, but insect behavior must be observed and studied. Much of it occurs underwater, shrouded by the environment, and unless you want to don oxygen tanks and wet suit, you'll need to rely on books such as this guide and the books relating to specific species listed in the reference section of each chapter. Your ability to match the behavior of an insect will depend on your ability to identify it, first, and then to read up on its behavior.

Much of the text of this guide is devoted to identification, but a large share of each chapter on the insect orders is given over to behavior. We feel it's essential to use specific tactics for each insect type. We've tried to simplify this approach by organizing the identification so that insects within an order are grouped by their behavior as well as their taxonomy. Again, using tactics based on insect behavior is as important to fishing success as using a pattern based on the appearance of the natural insects.

Making insect behavior even more important is the fact that it directly influences which insect out of hundreds of choices fish will feed on. The two factors of behavior most important to consider are availability and action.

Availability

No matter how abundant a particular insect might be, fish will not eat it unless it's available. The insect's stage of development, its habitat, and its daily level of activity all affect its availability.

Stage of Development

Nymphs/Larvae. Aquatic insects spend most of their life cycle in the nymph or larval stage. They are most abundant when they first hatch from the eggs, before their numbers are dwindled by disease and predation. But young nymphs and larvae are less available to fish than mature ones, because of their small size and ability to hide in the substrate. Their small size also means fish receive less energy by feeding on them. As nymphs and larvae mature, their availability generally increases along with their size. For these reasons mature nymphs and larvae are better to imitate than young ones. The maturity of nymphs or larvae can be gauged by their size and development. Nymphs (insects with incomplete metamorphosis) will develop dark, almost black, wing pads when mature. Larvae (insects with complete metamorphosis) show no signs of wing pads until they transform to the pupal stage, so size can be an important consideration.

Emergers. When nymphs or pupae reach their final level of development, they often become more active in the water as they get ready to emerge as adults. This activity further increases their availability to fish and their importance to the angler. The greatest availability often occurs during emergence when many nymphs and pupae rise to the surface. Fish take advantage of this activity by feeding heavily and selectively on the emerging insects.

Adults. Most adults offer themselves twice to feeding fish— first, when they escape the nymphal or pupal shuck on the water's surface, and second, when they return to the water to lay their eggs. The importance of adults during emergence depends on how quickly they fly off the water. Fish will usually concentrate on the rising nymphs or pupae when the adults escape quickly. If the adults sit on the surface long enough, however, fish will turn their attention to that form of the insect. Ovipositing (egg-laying) adults often become easy targets for fish. Most lay their eggs on the surface, and there they often die or get caught in the surface film. Others dive underwater and swim to the bottom to lay their eggs. In both cases they become readily available to fish. Imitating the appropriate behavior can provide excellent fishing.

Habitat

Where an insect lives also influences its availability. For example, some insects live under rocks or burrow into the bottoms of streams or lakes. These insects are rarely available to fish, except during emergence when they may leave the bottom and swim to the surface. Other insects live on top of rocks and bottom materials or even swim actively in open water. These insects are much more available and more important to imitate. Insects that live in fast water areas are also more likely to get washed into the current than those that live in slow water areas. Look carefully for this information in each of the chapters covering the insect orders. The following table summarizes the major habitat types utilized by the different orders of aquatic insects.

Insect Orders by Water Type

Fast to Moderate Currents		Moderate to Slow Currents		Still Water
Riffles	Runs	Flats	Pools	Lakes
MF	MF	MF	MF	MF
SF	SF			
		DF	DF	DF
		WB	WB	WB
		BT	BT	BT
CF	CF	CF	CF	CF
DP	DP	DP	DP	DP

Codes: MF—Mayflies; SF—Stoneflies; DF—Damselflies and Dragonflies; WB—Water Bugs; BT—Beetles; CF—Caddisflies; DP—Diptera

Daily Changes in Activity

Other, more subtle changes also affect insect availability. Changes in weather, water flows, and temperature interact in complex and poorly understood ways to affect insect activity. There is, however, one predictable daily cycle of insect activity important to the flyfisher—it's called *behavioral drift*. Insects in streams and rivers occasionally let go of the bottom and drift in the current for 10, 20, or more feet depending on current speed and bottom type. This activity apparently serves to disperse insects into all usable habitats and reduce competition for food and space. Many types of insects drift in this manner on a regular daily cycle, with peak drift occurring around sunrise and sunset and during the middle of the night.

Fishermen have long known that fishing in the early morning

or late evening can be better than mid-day. Behavioral drift is one possible reason. Knowing which insects are abundant in different sections of streams or rivers and fishing their imitations in the morning or evening can quickly improve your results.

Action

Once you have determined a particular insect is available to the fish, what action you give its pattern is determined by the behavior of the natural in the water. Most insects fall into one of three categories: clingers, crawlers, or swimmers (some insects are also burrowers, but burrowers are not available while under the substrate). Clingers and crawlers move awkwardly in open water and are best imitated with a slow or dead-drift retrieve. Swimmers, on the other hand, move easily through open water by using their tails, legs, or body for swimming. Swimmers should be imitated by twitching or stripping the fly during the retrieve. The speed of the retrieve will vary with the specific type of insect being imitated. The action of adults on the surface will also vary. At times adults sit motionless, while at other times they flutter or skate across the surface. Fish your fly with the same action as the natural.

The three steps listed below will help you use this Waterwise Guide to decide which are the best patterns and tactics for imitating different insects.

1. First, determine which insect is most available to fish. Do this by observing and collecting the insects from the area you are fishing. Use the keys in this guide to find out what insects are present.

2. Second, decide where the insect is available. For example, are fish taking it off the bottom, in mid-depths, or on the surface? Again, careful observation along with the information in this guidebook should help you make this determination.

3. Third, observe the behavior of the natural in the water or read about it in the appropriate section of this guidebook. Then, match the action you give the fly to that behavior.

Tactics

Choosing the right tactic is critical to presenting your fly with the action of the natural. Specific approaches needed will depend on the type of fly you're using and the type of water you're fishing.

Many books have been written that describe flyfishing techniques in great detail (see references at the end of this chapter). In the space available here, only a brief overview is possible. However, if the basic tactics outlined here are mastered, more complicated strategies can be easily incorporated into your bag of tricks. The methods described here are divided into those needed for streams and lakes.

The tactics have been numbered "1" through "10." **In the following chapters, tactics for imitating specific insects will be referred to by these numbers.** Remember, these are only general guidelines, especially in the tackle category.

Streams and Rivers

Streams and rivers are constantly affected by water currents; the type of bottom, shape of the channel, and kinds of insects found there are all products of the current. Likewise, your tactics in streams and rivers are constantly influenced by currents. At times, the currents will be an aide by adding life-like action to your fly. Other times, currents will be a hindrance by causing your fly to drag unnaturally. Because of the current, your presentations in streams or rivers will fall in one of two directions—upstream or downstream. Which direction is best will depend on what you want your fly to do.

Nymphs:

1. Upstream dead-drift with strike indicator. This is one of the most effective tactics for fishing a nymph naturally along the bottom of a riffle or run.

Tackle: Rod—8-9' for 5-7 wt. line; line—double taper floating; leader—8-12' tapered to 3x-5x with strike indicator; fly—nymph pattern, usually weighted.

Casting Position: Stand 10-30 feet downstream of the area you want to fish.

Casting Direction: Cast upstream or up and across so your fly lands four to eight feet above the area you want to cover.

Retrieve: A dead-drift retrieve is usually preferred. As your fly floats downstream it will sink quickly. To prevent drag and maintain control, strip in slack line with your free hand and gradually raise your rod tip. Retrieve fast enough to keep a taut line without moving the fly.

Special Notes: This technique, while often very effective, requires great concentration. The strike indicator is the key. Watch it for any unnatural movement. It may simply slow down or it may move sideways or dip into the water. Movements will generally be very slight, and you must strike instantly before the fish has time to spit out the fly. Closed-cell, self-adhesive indicators are available from a number of companies, but strike indicators can also be made of bright yarn, a one-inch length of orange floating fly line with the core removed, or a cork (1/8 to 1/4 inch in diameter) painted red or orange. As a general rule, place the indicator approximately twice the distance from the fly as the average depth of the water. Make adjustments to that distance depending on current speed.

2. Up and across or across dead-drift. This technique works best for fishing nymphs at mid-depth where they may be drifting or rising to hatch. When fish can be seen actively feeding below the surface, try this tactic.

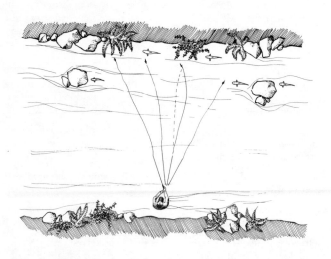

Tackle: Rod—8-9' for 4-6 wt. line; line—double taper floating or sink tip; leader—8-12' for floating line, 3-6' for sink-tip, tapered to 3x-5x; fly—nymph or wet fly, weighted or unweighted.

Casting Position: Stand 10-20 feet downstream and off to the side of the water being fished.

Casting Direction: Cast straight across or upstream at a 45 degree angle far enough above feeding fish so that you fly will have time to sink to the fish's level before it reaches them.

Retrieve: In most cases a dead-drift retrieve will produce best. To prevent drag, mend line up- or downstream as necessary. Raise your rod tip as the fly drifts toward you and lower it as the fly drifts away to keep the fly moving naturally and prevent slack line from forming.

Special Notes: Getting the fly to the level of the fish is the most important aspect of this tactic. Use weighted flies or a sink-tip line depending on depth and speed of the water being fished. Strikes will often be subtle, and a strike indicator can be used to detect them.

3. Down and across with twitches. This method presents the fly near the surface of the water and gives it a swimming action. It's best when active nymphs are swimming in the water or rising to hatch.

Tackle: Rod—8-9' for 4-6 wt. line; line—double taper floating; leader—8-12' tapered to 3x-5x; fly—nymph or wet fly.

Casting Position: Stand across from and slightly above the area to be fished.

Casting Direction: Cast across and slightly downstream so your fly will drift over visible fish or through suitable holding water.

Retrieve: Let the fly drift downstream without movement for several feet to give it time to sink below the surface. Mending the line may be necessary to prevent drag. When your fly reaches the fish or holding water, give it a swimming action by gently twitching the rod tip. Continue this action until the line has straightened out below you.

Special Notes: A strike indicator is rarely needed for this type of nymph fishing. Your fly will generally be within one or two feet of the surface, and strikes are often hard. Hesitate a second before setting the hook, or you may pull the fly out of the fish's mouth. Also, set the hook gently; pulling hard upstream as the fish turns downstream often results in a broken tippet.

Emergers:
4. Up and across dead-drift. This can be a deadly tactic for imitating emerging nymphs or pupae hanging in the surface film.

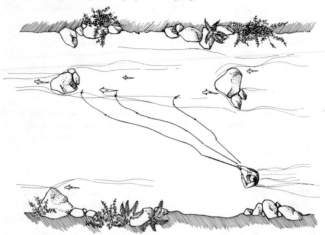

Tackle: Rod—7 1/2-9' for 4-6 wt. line; line—double taper floating; leader—8-12' tapered to 4x-6x; fly—floating nymph, soft hackle, or pupa.

Casting Position: Stand 10-30 feet downstream of and slightly to the side of the area being fished.

Casting Direction: Cast upstream or up and across, so the fly lands three to four feet above rising fish or holding water.

Retrieve: A dead-drift retrieve is generally best. Prevent drag with line mends and retrieve slack by lifting your rod tip as fly drifts towards you.

Special Notes: This is essentially dry fly fishing using a fly that is in or just below the surface film. It will generally prove most effective during a hatch when fish are taking nymphs or pupae near the surface. Dry flies may work at such times as well, but this method often produces more and larger fish. Avoid drag and present your fly to actively feeding fish. Strikes will typically be seen as surface swirls or flashes just under the water.

5. Down and across with lift. This is the most effective method of imitating nymphs or pupae that rise actively to the surface during emergence.

Tackle: Rod—7 1/2-9' for 4-6 wt. line; line—double taper floating; leader—8-12' tapered to 4x-6x; fly—soft hackle, flymph, or wet fly.

Casting Position: Stand just upstream (5-15 feet) and to one side of the area being fished.

Casting Direction: Your cast may vary from straight across to down and across at a 45 degree angle.

Retrieve: This method requires a more active retrieve to imitate the swimming motion of the natural. Give your fly time to sink six inches to a foot deep, while mending line to prevent drag if necessary. When the fly approaches feeding fish or holding areas, tease the fly to the surface by gently lifting your rod tip. If no fish strikes, drop your rod tip and repeat the lift one or two more times if possible.

Special Notes: When caddis emerge, the pupae often swim vigorously to the surface. This tactic, also called the Leisenring lift, imitates the action of caddis or other active swimmers perfectly.

Dry Flies:
6. Upstream or up and across. This is the most common method for fishing dry flies. It works best for imitating naturals that float with little or no motion on the surface.

Tackle: Rod—7 1/2-9' for a 3-6 wt. line; line—double taper floating; leader—8-12' tapered to 4x-6x; fly—any type of floating fly.

Casting Position: Stand 10-30 feet downstream of and slightly to one side of the water being fished.

Casting Direction: Cast straight upstream or upstream and across. Cast should be made so that the line and leader are not over the fish's "window" (field of view).

Retrieve: A dead-drift retrieve without drag produces the best results in most situations. Drag can be avoided by mending your fly line up- or downstream. Take up slack line as your fly drifts toward you by stripping in line and lifting your rod tip. Short casts of 15-30 feet will make line control much easier.

Special Notes: The dry fly fished upstream has been the preferred method of flyfishing purists for centuries. Its effectiveness has maintained its popularity. This method can be used for searching water or when fish are feeding actively on the surface. By standing below the fish, you won't spook them as easily, but be careful not to cast your line or leader over the fish.

7. Downstream or down and across. This alternative method of presenting dry flies works well for imitating insects that flutter or skate over the surface or for dead-drifting presentations on flat smooth waters.

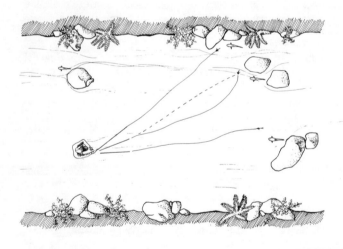

Tackle: Rod—7 1/2-9' for 3-6 wt. line; line—double taper floating; leader—8-12' tapered to 4x-6x; fly—any type of floating fly.

Casting Position: Stand 15-40 feet upstream of and slightly to the side of the area being fished.

Casting Direction: Cast downstream or down and across with a slack line cast. Present your fly one to three feet upstream and in front of rising fish.

Retrieve: This method allows you to use either an active twitching retrieve or a dead-drift presentation. Twitch your fly by letting your line tighten below you, then lift your rod tip high and twitch it gently.

Special Notes: During heavy hatches on flats and smooth waters, this method will often out-fish the upstream presentation, since the fly always drifts over the fish before the line or leader does. You will be wading above fish with this tactic, so your approach must be quiet and delicate.

Lakes

The lack of current in lakes requires that you supply all the action to the fly while fishing it. You must also present your fly at the proper depth and in the area of the lake where fish are feeding. Weed beds, submerged wood debris, and shoals are key areas. Depending on the natural being imitated, fish lakes with one of the three tactics suggested here.

8. Dead-drift. This method works well for many situations on lakes. It can be used when imitating slowly rising nymphs or pupae, or for drifting dry flies on the surface.

Tackle: Rod—8-9 1/2' for 5-7 wt. line; line—double taper or weight forward floating or sink-tip; leader—8-20' tapered to 3x-6x; fly— nymph, wet fly, or dry fly.

Casting Position/Direction: A slight breeze will aide this tactic. Cast perpendicular to the direction of the wind, then simply let the breeze drift your line across the surface. Present your fly where fish are feeding. Pay close attention to weed beds, shoals, and drop-offs.

Retrieve: Whether fishing deep with a nymph or on the surface, use a slow hand-twist retrieve. Retrieve just fast enough to keep slack out of the line.

Special Notes: Many midges, mayflies, and slow moving caddisflies are imitated with this method. Nymphs and pupae may be fished near the surface or close to the bottom depending on the feeding position of the fish. Finding the right depth can be critical.

9. Strip Retrieve. The strip retrieve best imitates nymphs or adults that move actively in or on the water.

Tackle: Rod—8-9 1/2' for a 5-8 wt. line; line—weight forward floating, sink-tip, or full-sink; leader—8-12' for floating line, 3-8' for full sink-tip or full sink, tapered to 3x-6x; fly—nymph, pupa, or dry fly.

Casting Position/Direction: In most cases you will be fishing along weed beds, submerged logs, or drop-offs when using this method. Cast near structures and let the fly sink close to the bottom when imitating most nymphs and pupae.

Retrieve: Your fly should be retrieved in strips or jerks by pulling in line with your free hand. The length and speed of the strips will vary depending on the action of the natural. Pausing several seconds between strips can also be important.

Special Notes: Many lake insects move with a swimming motion. This method will imitate most of them. Swimming mayflies, caddisfly pupae, dragonfly nymphs, and leeches are common underwater forms that swim. Use the full-sinking line when you want to keep the fly on the bottom. Travelling sedge adults (caddisflies) are the most common insects that move actively on the surface.

10. Pull Retrieve. This is a variation of the strip retrieve. It should be used when naturals move in a steady swimming motion instead of in short spurts.

Tackle: Same as #9, "Strip Retrieve".

Casting Position/Direction: Same as #9, "Strip Retrieve".

Retrieve: With this method, retrieve your fly with a long even pull. Combine pulling in line with your free hand while slowly lifting your rod tip. The speed of retrieve is very important so try a slower or faster retrieve if you're unsuccessful at first.

Special Notes: Some caddis pupae rise to the surface with a steady swimming motion. Damselflies, scuds, midges, and water boatmen are others that are imitated well with this tactic.

References
The books listed here are but a sampling of the good texts devoted to flyfishing tactics. New titles are published every year that are worthy of your attention.

Anderson, Sheridan. *The Curtis Creek Manifesto*. Portland, Oregon: Frank Amato Publications, 1976.

Brooks, Charles. *Larger Trout for the Western Fly Fisherman*. Tulsa, Oklahoma: Winchester Press, 1983.

Brooks, Charles. *Nymph Fishing for Larger Trout*. New York: Crown, 1976.

Gierach, John. *Flyfishing the High Country*. Boulder, Colorado: Pruett Press, 1985.

Gordon, Sid. *How to Fish from Top to Bottom*. Harrisburg, Pennsylvania: Stackpole Books, 1978.

Kaufmann, Randall, and Ronald Cordes. *Lake Fishing with a Fly*. Portland, Oregon: Frank Amato Publications, 1985.

LaFontaine, Gary. *The Challenge of the Trout*. Missoula, Montana: Mountain Press, 1976.

Migel, J. Michael, ed. *Masters on the Dry Fly*. Farmingdale, New York: Brown Book Co., 1977.

Quick, Jim. *Fishing the Nymph*. Books Demand, UMI.

Sawyer, Frank. *Nymphs and the Trout*. New York: Crown Publishers, 1973.

Swisher, Doug, and Carl Richards. *Fly Fishing Strategy*. New York: Crown, 1975.

Wright, Leonard. *Fly Fishing Heresies*. S. Hackensack, New Jersey: Stoeger Publishing Co.

4. Beginning Identification

You've just collected an insect. Perhaps you found it underwater on some rocks or floating on the water's surface. Maybe you caught it in mid-air. Now you want to know what it is. This chapter will help you find out.

First make sure it's an insect. (You may wish to review Chapter 1 for more details on insect anatomy.) Check to see if it has the following characteristics:

— One pair of antennae.
— Three distinct body regions: head, thorax, and abdomen.
— Three pairs of jointed legs on the thorax.
— No jointed legs on the abdomen (short unjointed prolegs may be present).

Even this apparently simple test may lead you astray. Adults, nymphs, and pupae will have those characteristics, but many larvae have greatly reduced antennae and heads, reduced or absent thoracic legs, and indistinctly differentiated body regions. These larvae are more worm-like than insect-like in appearance. If you're not sure you have an insect, try the keys in this chapter. If none of the descriptions fit, you probably have a round worm, flat worm, or leech instead of an insect larva.

Begin your identification with the Key to Life Stages. This key will determine if you have a nymph, larva, pupa, or adult insect. (Of course, if you already know what stage the insect is in, you can skip this key and proceed to the next level of keys.) You'll next want to determine what insect order your specimen belongs to. Go to the key indicated by the Key to Life Stages. This key will tell you what order of insect you have (mayfly, stonefly, caddisfly, etc.) and where to proceed in the guide for final identification and more detailed information.

Until you learn the terms used in the keys, you may have to refer to the section on insect anatomy in Chapter 1 or to the glossary given at the end of the book.

Not all the insects you collect along a stream or lake will be of aquatic origin. Many terrestrial insects live near the water and frequently fall into it. Since this field guide covers only aquatic insects, trying to identify a terrestrial insect with these keys will cause confusion. To prevent possible problems, follow these guidelines:

— Live insects collected underwater are almost always aquatic species. Terrestrial insects tend to float in the surface film when they fall into the water.

— Most aquatic insects show distinct adaptations to living in the water; for example, gills, tails, swimming hairs on legs, or a streamlined or flat shape normally indicate the insect is aquatic. Also, if the insect appears to struggle in the water, rather than move or float comfortably, it's probably a terrestrial insect.

— The orders that contain both terrestrial and aquatic species cause the most problems. The orders listed below contain terrestrial species commonly found near the water. Those orders preceded by an asterisk contain both aquatic and terrestrial species.

*Beetles (Order Coleoptera), *True Flies (Order Diptera), Ants and Wasps (Order Hymenoptera), *Moths and Butterflies (Order Lepidoptera), Grasshoppers and Crickets (Order Orthoptera), *True Bugs (Order Hemiptera)

Insects of the orders containing both types of insects are most likely terrestrial insects if they struggle in the water and do not fit the descriptions in the keys properly.

Key to Life Stages

This simple key will help you determine the life stage (nymph, larva, pupa, or adult) of any insect you might find. After determining which life stage the insect is in, you'll be directed to the key that will help you identify it to order.

1a. If there are 2 or 4 fully developed wings (though fore wings may be hard, shell-like, and cover hind wings)* or partially developed wings in wing pads (not visible on very young specimens), go to **2**.

1b. If wings and wing pads are completely absent* (note: jointed legs may or may not be present), it is a LARVA. Go to p. 46.

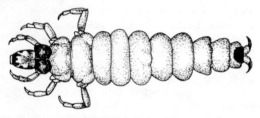

2a. If there are fully developed, (usually) conspicuous wings, or there are wings but fore wings are hard, shell-like, and cover hind wings; and if there are three pairs of jointed legs, it is an ADULT. Go to p. 52.

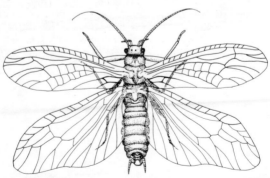

2b. If wings are only partially developed in pouch-like wing pads (not visible on very young specimens), go to **3**.

3a. If wings are partially developed in wing pads and there are freely movable legs; and if insects are active and not found in cocoons or cases, it is a **NYMPH**. Go to p. 46.

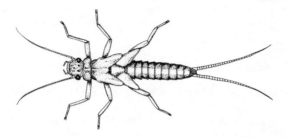

3b. If wings are partially developed but legs are fused to body or free but close to body, and insects are typically inactive and sometimes found in cocoons or sealed in cases, it is a **PUPA**. Go to p. 50.

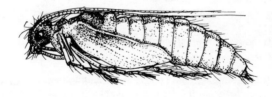

* Note: The wings of some adults (some stoneflies, for example) may be reduced or absent. While these specimens may resemble nymphs or larvae, they will be found on land instead of underwater.

Key to Nymphs and Larvae

This key will lead you to the order of the insect you have identified as a nymph or larva. Some of the identifications in this key depend on close inspection of the insect. A loupe or hand magnifying lens is recommended.

1a. If you identified the insect as a nymph using the Key to Life Stages, go to **2**.

1b. If you identified it as a larva, go to **6**.

2a. If mouthparts are beak- or needle-like and suited for sucking, and insect was found skating on the surface or diving and swimming actively underwater, it is a WATER BUG. Go to p. 113.

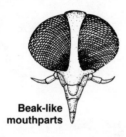

Beak-like mouthparts

2b. If mouthparts are designed for chewing and are not needle-like, go to **3**.

3a. If lower lip (labium) forms an extendable, arm-like structure that is longer than head when extended, it is a DRAGONFLY or DAMSELFLY. Go to p. 97.

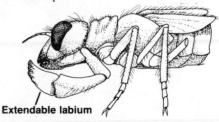

Extendable labium

3b. If labium is small and does not extend, go to **4**.

4a. If abdomen ends with three slender tails, and gills, typically plate-like, are located on sides of abdomen; and if legs end in a single claw, it is a MAYFLY. Go to p. 57.

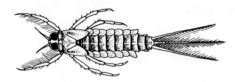

4b. If abdomen ends with two tails, go to **5**.

5a. If gills are plate-like and located on sides of abdomen, and legs end in a single claw, it is a MAYFLY. Go to p. 57.

5b. If gills are absent or, if present, are finger-like or thickly branched and are found on underside of head or thorax; and if legs end in two claws, it is a STONEFLY. Go to p. 76.

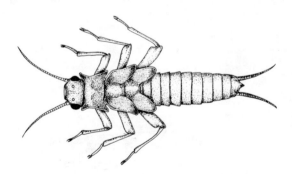

6a. If there are three pairs of jointed legs on the thorax, go to **7**.

6b. If thorax has no jointed legs (but fleshy, unjointed protuberances or prolegs may be present on thorax and/or abdomen), go to **10**.

7a. If there are at least two pairs of unjointed fleshy prolegs tipped with tiny hooks (crochets) present on abdomen, and insect is typically found covered by a silk blanket on sides of rocks, it is an **AQUATIC MOTH**. Go to p. 172.

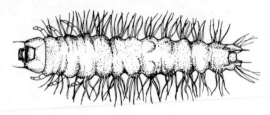

7b. If abdomen has no prolegs, go to **8**.

8a. If last abdominal segment bears 2 small- to moderate-sized hooks (anal hooks), and antennae are minute (invisible to unaided eye); and if gills, when present, are seldom confined to sides of the abdomen, and larvae are free-living or live in cases made of sand, gravel, or plant material, is a **CADDISFLY**. Go to p. 129.

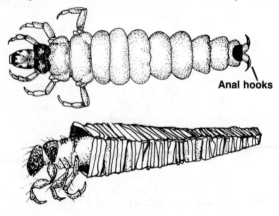

Anal hooks

8b. If abdomen ends with 4 anal hooks, or anal hooks are absent; and if gills, when present, are restricted to sides of abdomen, go to **9**.

9a. If first 7 or 8 abdominal segments each have a pair of lateral gill filaments, and the last segment has 4 anal hooks or a single tapered filament, it is an ALDERFLY/HELLGRAMMITE. Go to p. 120.

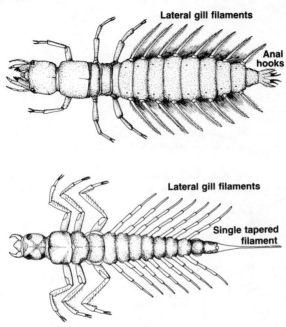

9b. If end of the abdomen is without hooks or filament, and lateral abdominal gills are present or absent, it is a BEETLE. Go to p. 166.

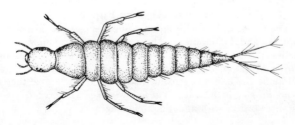

10a. If head capsule is absent, and body is maggot-like, usually elongated and cylindrical, it is one of the TRUE FLIES. Go to p. 154.

10b. If a distinct head capsule is present (note: it may be withdrawn inside first thoracic segment), go to **11**.

11a. If rear of body is simple, without long hairs, gills, prolegs, or breathing tubes, it is a BEETLE. Go to p. 166.

11b. If rear of body has long hairs, gills, prolegs, breathing tubes, or a combination of these, it is one of the TRUE FLIES. Go to p. 154.

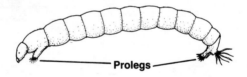

Prolegs

Key to Aquatic Pupae

The major orders with aquatic pupal stages are Trichoptera, Diptera, and Lepidoptera. The mature larvae of most aquatic beetles (Order Coleoptera) and all alderflies and dobsonflies (Order Megaloptera) leave the water to form pupal cells in damp soil along the banks of streams and lakes. Their pupae therefore do not develop in the water. The following key will serve to separate the three orders with aquatic pupal stages.

1a. If there is one pair of wing pads, and antennae are much shorter than body; and if head lacks long, curved mandibles but projecting gills or breathing tubes are often found on thorax or tip of abdomen; and if legs are either free or fused to body, it is one of the TRUE FLIES. Go to p. 154.

1b. If there are 2 pairs of wing pads, and insect is found in case or cocoon, go to **2**.

2a. If legs and antennae are free, not fused to body, and antennae are as long as or longer than body; and if insect is found in case of sand, gravel, or plant material, and front of head has long, curved mandibles which project forward, it is a CADDISFLY. Go to p. 129.

Antennae

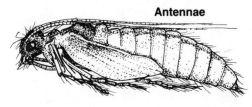

2b. If legs and antennae are fused to body, and antennae are shorter than body; and if insect is found in silken cocoon, and long, curved mandibles are absent, it is an AQUATIC MOTH. Go to p. 172.

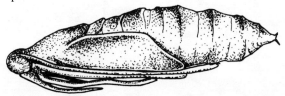

Key to Aquatic Adults

This key will lead you to the order of the insect you have identified as an adult. Some of the identifications in this key depend on close inspection of the insect. A loupe or hand magnifying lens is recommended.

1a. If front wings are leathery or hard, forming a cover over the hind wings and abdomen (note: such adults may appear wingless, but by lifting up the thick front wings, the hind wings can be easily seen), go to **2**.

1b. If front wings are entirely membranous, go to **3**.

2a. If mouthparts are beak- or needle-like, designed for sucking, and the insect is found on water's surface or diving and swimming actively underwater, it is a WATER BUG. Go to p. 113.

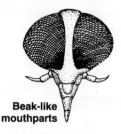

**Beak-like
mouthparts**

2b. If mouthparts are not needle-like but are, instead, designed for chewing, and the insect is sometimes found on water's surface but is more commonly found swimming actively underwater, it is a BEETLE. Go to p. 166.

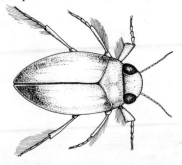

3a. If there is one pair of wings, go to **4**.

3b. If there are 2 pairs of wings, go to **5**.

4a. If abdomen has 2 or 3 long tails, and when at rest, wings are held upright, not flat over abdomen; and if thorax is without halteres (modified hind wings), it is a **MAYFLY**. Go to p. 57.

4b. If abdomen has no tails, and wings normally rest on top of abdomen; and if halteres are present on thorax, it is one of the **TRUE FLIES**. Go to p. 154.

5a. If wings and body are covered with small flattened scales, and mouthparts usually form a long coiled tube, it is an AQUATIC MOTH. Go to p. 172.

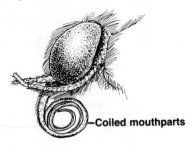

—Coiled mouthparts

5b. If wings and body are not covered with scales (though they may be covered with fine hairs), and mouthparts do not form a long coiled tube, go to **6**.

6a. If wings are covered with fine hairs obscuring venation and when at rest are held tent-like over abdomen, and antennae are as long as or longer than body, it is a CADDISFLY. Go to p. 129.

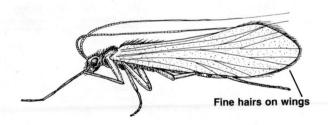

Fine hairs on wings

6b. If wings are not covered with hairs, making venation visible, and wing shape and antennae length are variable, go to **7**.

7a. If hind wings are distinctly smaller than front wings, and wings stand upright when at rest; and if abdomen has 2 or 3 long tails, it is a MAYFLY. Go to p. 57.

7b. If hind wings are as large as or larger than front wings, go to **8**.

8a. If antennae are short, slender, and inconspicuous, and eyes are very large; and if abdomen is typically long and slender, it is one of the **DRAGONFLIES** or **DAMSELFLIES**. Go to p. 97. .

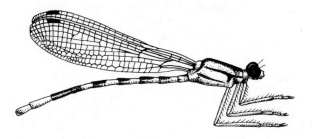

8b. If antennae are well-developed and conspicuous, and eyes are moderate to small in size, go to **9**.

9a. If abdomen ends in 2 tails of various lengths (sometimes very short and difficult to see), and tarsi are 2- or 3-segmented; and if wings lie flat over abdomen when at rest, it is a STONEFLY. Go to p. 76.

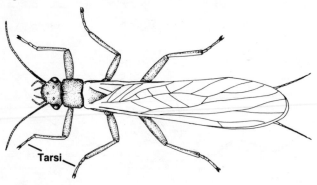

9b. If abdomen has no tails, and tarsi are 5-segmented; and if wings lie tent-like or flat over abdomen when at rest, it is an ALDERFLY or DOBSONFLY. Go to p. 120.

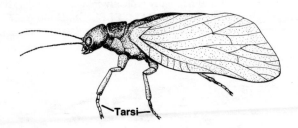

5. Mayflies: Order Ephemeroptera

Key to Mayfly Nymphs, p. 61
Key to Mayfly Adults, p. 64

Mayflies and flyfishing are so closely linked it's hard to imagine one without the other. The abundance, availability, and behavior of mayflies have made them a major influence on flyfishing throughout its history. This chapter provides keys for identifying nymph and adult mayflies and describes which patterns and tactics to use.

Basic Identification and Similar Orders

Mayfly nymphs are easily recognized by the following three major features: 1) plate-like gills on the sides of the abdominal segments; 2) a single claw at the end of each leg; and 3) three long tails (only two for some species). Nymphs most frequently confused with mayflies are stonefly and damselfly nymphs.

Adult mayflies are unique. Their large front wings, held upright when at rest, plus their long, delicate tails give adult mayflies a distinctive look. In flight, mayflies may be confused with caddis adults— the long antennae of caddis sometimes appear to be the tails of a mayfly. Mayflies, however, typically fly slower and less erratically than caddisflies, and the tails of mayflies do not lie back over the body like the antennae of caddisflies.

The following table will help you distinguish insects easily confused with mayflies:

Nymphs

Identifying Characters	Mayflies	Stoneflies	Damselflies
Wing Pads	4, but only 2 visible	4, visible on mature nymphs	4, visible on mature nymphs

Gills	Plate-like gills on sides of abdomen	Gills absent or filamentous gills on underside of thorax or head	3 tail-like gills on tip of abdomen
Tails	3, sometimes 2	2	3 flat gills that appear as tails
Claws Per Leg	1	2	2

Adults

Identifying Characters	**Mayflies**	**Stoneflies**	**Caddisflies**
Wings	4, sometimes only 2; hind wings much smaller than fore wings; wings typically held straight up	4, lie flat on top of abdomen	4, held tent-shaped over abdomen
Tails	2 or 3 long tails	2, ranging from body length to very short	None
Antennae	Short, usually less than width of head	Almost body length	Body length or longer

Size Range

The great variety of mayflies gives them a wide range of sizes. Mature nymphs and adults (excluding tails) may range from 3-35mm (1/8"-1 1/2") or, in hook sizes, from a #26 to a #6 3XL. Even though there's a wide range of sizes, most species are 6-12mm (1/4"-1/2") long. This equals a range of hook sizes (Mustad 94833, for example) from #16 to #10.

Life Cycle

Mayflies have incomplete metamorphosis, meaning they pass through egg, nymph, and adult stages. The adult or winged stage consists of two phases, the subimago (commonly called the dun) and the imago (commonly called the spinner). The dun is the winged form that emerges from the nymph. It's not a true adult because it can't mate in this stage. Duns can be recognized by the smokey, opaque color of their wings. After a short time (anywhere from one or two hours to several days), the dun molts by shedding its exoskeleton and becomes a spinner. Spinners have clear, glass-like wings. It is the spinner that forms mating swarms and lays eggs. Mayflies are the only known insect to molt in a winged stage.

The majority of mayflies have a one-year life cycle. Development time for each stage is summarized below.

Stage	Average Duration	Extremes
Egg	1-3 months	Several seconds (Baetidae: *Callibaetis* sp.) to 8-9 months (Polymitarcydae: *Ephoron* sp.)
Nymph	8-11 months	3-4 weeks (Siphlonuridae: *Parameletus columbiae*) to 2 years (Ephemeridae: *Hexagenia limbata*)
Dun (Subimago)	1-3 days	1-3 hours
Spinner (Imago)	1-2 days	2-3 hours (Caenidae: *Brachycercus* sp.) to 3-4 weeks (Baetidae: *Callibaetis* sp.)

The majority of the life cycle is spent in the nymphal form. During their development, nymphs may molt 20-30 times. Because nymphs are the longest-lived stage, they are always available to fish to some extent and are a frequent part of the fish's diet where they occur.

Emergence from nymph to the dun most often occurs in the surface film. Some species also emerge underwater or on land. During a hatch, rising nymphs and duns floating on the surface can result in selective feeding by fish.

Male spinners form large aerial swarms. When a female flies into the swarm, mating occurs in the air. After mating, females begin laying eggs. Most females release several clusters of eggs on the surface film, but some species crawl underwater where they attach clumps of eggs on the bottom. Individual females may lay from several hundred to several thousand eggs.

"Spinner falls" occur when spent females fall on the water's surface and die. Fish feed selectively on these dead and dying insects during spinner falls. Late evening and early morning are the times a flyfisherman is most likely to find fish rising to spinners. A spent-wing spinner pattern matching the size and color of the insect is the best choice at these times.

North American Distribution and Abundance

Region	# of Families	# of Genera
East	16	47
Central	14	46
West	12	50
Total in N.A.	18	69

Approximate number of North American species: 570

Habitat Preferences

Mayflies are common in most freshwater habitats that have suitable water quality. Mayflies are sensitive to water pollution, but different species can tolerate different types or amounts of pollution. Thus, mayflies can be useful indicators of water quality if carefully studied.

Mayflies occur in both flowing and still waters. While they can be important to flyfishers in both streams and lakes, their greatest diversity and abundance occurs in streams. Mayfly nymphs are common in mountain streams 10,000 feet above sea level as well as in warm, mud-bottom rivers near sea level. This adaptability means flyfishermen in every part of the country will find mayflies present and often important in their local waters.

Identification

The following keys divide all the mayflies into four groups: swimmers, crawlers, clingers, and burrowers. These four groups are based on the behavior of the nymphs.

Insect behavior is of major importance to flyfishers. By dividing all mayflies into four groups, not only is their identification greatly simplified, but much of the difficulty of pattern selection and presentation is eliminated.

More specific information on each of the four groups is presented following the keys.

Key to Mayfly Nymphs

In determining which type of mayfly nymph you've collected, consider first the overall body shape and the size of the head in relation to the body.

1a. If body and head are flattened, and head is wider than abdomen (excluding gills), it is CLINGER. Go to p. 71.

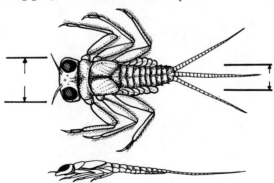

1b. If body and head are not flattened (though they may be slightly depressed), and width of head is equal to or less than width of abdomen (excluding gills), go to **2**.

2a. If body is round and streamlined, and edges of tails are fringed with fine hairs; and if oval gills are positioned on sides of abdomen (not forked or positioned on top of abdomen), it is a SWIMMER. Go to p. 67.

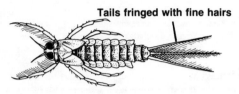

Tails fringed with fine hairs

2b. If body is not streamlined, and gills are either forked or oval and often positioned on top of abdomen, go to **3**.

3a. If gills are forked, and their margins fringed; and if mandibles form tusks visible from above, it is a BURROWER. Go to p. 73.

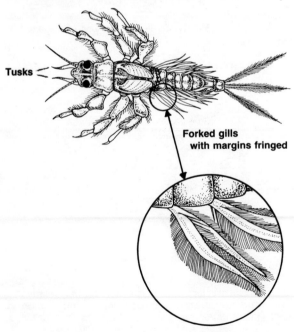

Tusks

Forked gills with margins fringed

3b. If gills are forked, and their margins are not fringed; or if gills are oval and positioned on top of abdomen, and tusk-like mandibles are missing (except a few species), it is a **CRAWLER**. Go to p. 69.

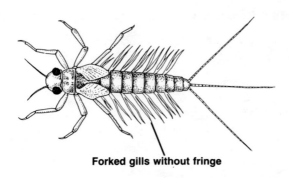

Forked gills without fringe

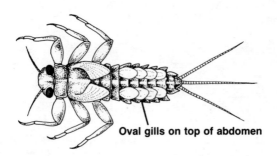

Oval gills on top of abdomen

Key to Mayfly Adults

Identification of mayfly adults (duns and spinners) begins with the number of tails present. To further identify the insect, you'll need to be familiar with anatomical terms discussed in Chapter 1.

1a. If the insect has two tails, go to **2**.

1b. If the insect has three tails, go to **4**.

2a. If head appears flat when viewed from side, and hind tarsi are distinctly 5-segmented; and if cubital intercalaries consist of 2 pairs, it is a CLINGER. Go to p. 71.

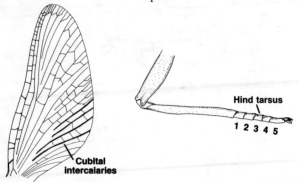

2b. If the insect does not have those characteristics, go to **3**.

3a. If body size (excluding tails) is large, 16-35mm (5/8"-1 3/8"), and hind wings are large, almost half the size of fore wings; and if abdomen has distinct dark markings, and fore wings show base of veins MP2 and CuA strongly diverging from base of vein MP1, it is a BURROWER. Go to p. 73.

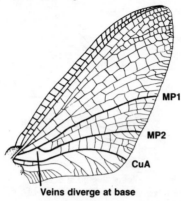

Veins diverge at base

3b. If body size is smaller, not over 17mm (5/8"), and hind wing size varies from very small (sometimes absent) to less than half as large as fore wings; and if base of veins MP2 and CuA do not diverge from base of MP1, it is a SWIMMER. Go to p. 67.

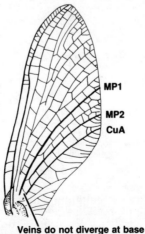

Veins do not diverge at base

4a. If body size (excluding tails) is large, 16-35mm (5/8"-1 3/8"), and hind wings are large, almost half as large as fore wings; and if abdomen has distinct dark markings, and fore wings show base of veins MP2 and CuA strongly diverging from base of vein MP1, it is a BURROWER. Go to p. 73.

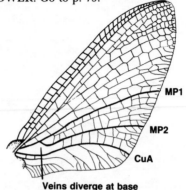

Veins diverge at base

4b. If body size is smaller, not over 17mm (5/8"), and hind wing size varies from very small (sometimes absent) to less than half as large as fore wings; and if base of wing veins MP2 and CuA do not diverge from base of MP1, it is a CRAWLER. Go to p. 69.

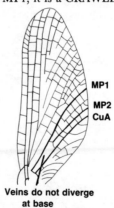

**Veins do not diverge
at base**

Swimmers

Major families and genera of swimmers:

Families	Genera (# of species)
Baetidae	*Baetis* (41)
	Callibaetis (23)
	Pseudocleon (19)
Siphlonuridae	*Siphlonurus* (17)
	Ameletus (31)
	Isonychia (25)

Swimmer nymphs are easily recognized by their slender, tapered bodies, slender legs, and three tails (one species has only two) with a fringe of fine interconnecting hairs that form a paddle-like surface. Swimmers may be as small as 4mm (1/8") or as large as nearly 25mm (1"). Swimmer adults have only two tails, and their hind wings range from quite small (Baetidae) to nearly half as large as the fore wings (Siphlonuridae).

Swimmers are abundant in habitats ranging from fast gravelly riffles at 10,000 feet to slow moving streams and lakes. The Speckle-Winged Quill (Baetidae: *Callibaetis* sp.) produces excellent mayfly hatches in lakes throughout North America, while the small Blue-Winged Olive (Baetidae: *Baetis* sp.) is equally important in streams.

Swimmers, as you might suspect, swim well. They dart through the water by rapidly flicking their abdomen and tail up and down. Their abundance and active behavior make them common food items. Their importance as food is further enhanced by their propensity to drift in stream currents, thus increasing their availability. This drift activity is particularly heavy at sunrise and sunset and occurs on a regular daily cycle. Nymph patterns should be tied slender and fished with a darting, twitching action near weedbeds, roots, boulders, and undercut banks.

Swimmers emerge in the surface film (Baetidae) or crawl out of the water on sticks or grass (Siphlonuridae). Emerger and dun patterns are excellent for the species that emerge in the surface film. Many species produce large spinner falls, making the spinner stage important to imitate at such times. The Gray or Black Drake (Siphlonuridae: *Siphlonurus* sp.), Blue-Winged Olive, and Speckle-Winged Quill produce some of the most important hatches of swimmers.

Major Hatches of Swimmers

Name	Emergence	Size	Dist.
Blue-Winged Olive Baetidae: *Baetis*	Mar-Nov	N: 3-12mm A: 3-10mm	E C W
Speckle-Winged Quill Baetidae: *Callibaetis*	Apr-Oct	N: 6-12mm A: 6-12mm	E C W
Tiny Blue-Winged Olive Baetidae: *Pseudocleon*	Jun-Aug	N: 3-9mm A: 3-9mm	E C W
Black or Gray Drake Siphlonuridae: *Siphlonurus*	Apr-Oct	N: 12-17mm A: 12-15mm	E C W
(No common name) Siphlonuridae: *Ameletus*	Apr-Oct	N: 6-14mm A: 10-14mm	W
White-Gloved Howdy Siphlonuridae: *Isonychia*	Jun-Sep	N: 12-15mm A: 12-15mm	E C W

Major Patterns and Tactics for Swimmers

Stage	Patterns	Ref.	Tactic
Nymph	Black Drake	2	2 or 3
	Little Olive	8	
Emerger	Floating Emerger Nymph	2	4
	Little Olive	2	
Dun	Blue-Winged Olive	2	6
	Adams	2, 8	
	Compara-Dun	2	
Spinner	Compara-Spinner	2	7

(Note: See p. 28 for information on references and p. 32 for information on tactics.)

Crawlers

Major familes and genera of crawlers:

Families	**Genera (# of species)**
Ephemerellidae	*Attenella* (4)
	Drunella (15)
	Ephemerella (28)
	Serratella (14)
Tricorythodidae	*Tricorythodes* (13)
Caenidae	*Caenis* (13)
Leptophlebiidae	*Leptophlebia* (10)
	Paraleptophlebia (33)

Crawler nymphs can be recognized by their rather square head and rectangular body, long forked gills (in Leptophlebiidae) or small gills on top of the abdomen (in Ephemerellidae, Tricorythodidae, and Caenidae), and three tails with fine whorls of hair rather than a fringe of interconnecting hair as in the swimmers. Adult crawlers all have three tails. Crawlers vary in size from the minute *Tricorythodes* (4mm, 1/8" or less) to the large *Drunella* (18mm, 3/4").

Crawlers are mayflies of streams and rivers; only the family Caenidae and some Tricorythodidae commonly occur in lakes. Crawlers are abundant in a wide variety of river habitats. Fast riffles, smooth runs, slow silty stretches, and thickly vegetated spring creeks all support good populations. The family Ephemerellidae contains many species that produce excellent hatches.

Nymphs spend most of their lives crawling quietly along the bottom, where they feed on algae and decaying vegetation. If they get washed into the current, they feebly try to swim back to the bottom. Nymph patterns are thus best fished dead drift near the bottom.

Emergence of crawlers occurs in shallow water near the shoreline (Leptophlebiidae and some Tricorythodidae) or underwater so that the duns float to the surface (most Ephemerellidae and some Tricorythodidae). Wet flies and emerger patterns fished near the surface produce well during hatches because of their similarity to the rising duns. Once on the surface, crawler duns tend to float long distances before flying. Spinner falls can also be heavy. This creates excellent dry-fly fishing with either dun or spinner patterns.

Major Hatches of Crawlers

Name	Emergence	Size	Dist.
Dark Hendrickson Ephemerellidae *Ephemerella subvaria*	Apr-Jun	N: 10-12mm A: 10-12mm	E C
Light Hendrickson Ephemerellidae *Ephemerella rotunda*	Mar-Jun	N: 8-10mm A: 8-10mm	E C
Pale Evening Dun Ephemerellidae *Ephemerella dorothea*	Apr-Jul	N: 7-9mm A: 7-9mm	E C
Large Blue-Winged Olive Ephemerellidae *Drunella cornuta*	May-Jun	N: 7-10mm A: 7-10mm	E C
Little Dark Hendrickson Ephemerellidae *Serratella deficiens*	Jun-Aug	N: 6-8mm A: 6-8mm	E C
Pale Morning Dun Ephemerellidae *Ephemerlla inermis, infrequens*	May-Aug	N: 7-9mm A: 7-9mm	W
Western Green Drake Ephemerellidae *Drunella grandis*	Jun-Jul	N: 11-15mm A: 11-15mm	W
Small Western Green Drake Ephemerellidae *Drunella flavilinea*	Jun-Aug	N: 7-9mm A: 7-9mm	W
Slate-Winged Olive Ephemerellidae *Drunella coloradensis*	Jul-Sep	N: 9-11mm A: 9-11mm	W

Name	Emergence	Size	Dist.
Small Western Hendrickson Ephemerellidae *Serratella tibialis*	Jul-Sep	N: 7-9mm A: 7-9mm	W
Slate-Winged Mahogany Dun Leptophlebiidae *Paraleptophlebia*	Apr-May and Aug-Sep	N: 7-9mm A: 7-9mm	E C W
Trico Tricorythodidae *Tricorythodes*	Jul-Oct	N: 3-5mm A: 3-5mm	E C W

Major Patterns and Tactics for Crawlers

Stage	Patterns	Ref.	Tactics
Nymph	Dark Green Drake	8	1 or 2
	Pheasant Tail	2, 8	
	Dark Hendrickson	8	
Emerger	Dark Cahill Wet	2	4
	Floating Emerger Nymph	2	
	Green Drake Emerger	7	4 or 5
Dun	Thorax Hendrickson	2	6 or 7
	Light Cahill	2, 8	
	Compara-Dun	2	
Spinner	Compara-Spinner	2	7
	Trico Poly Wing Spinner	2	

(Note: See p. 28 for information on references and p. 32 for information on tactics.)

Clingers

Major families and genera of clingers:

Families	Genera (# of species)
Heptageniidae	*Cinygmula* (11)
	Epeorus (19)
	Heptagenia (13)
	Rhithrogena (21)
	Stenonema (17)
	Stenacron (7)

All clingers belong to the family Heptageniidae. Nymphs are flattened dorsal-ventrally (from top to bottom), have prominent eyes on top of a broad, flat head, have relatively large plate-like gills, and have two (*Epeorus*) or three tails with few hairs. Like the nymphs, adults have flat heads when viewed from the side, but they have only two tails. The distinctive wing venation (see Key to Mayfly Adults) is the best way to recognize clinger adults.

Clingers occur only in streams and prefer moderate to fast riffle areas. Generally speaking, as current speed dwindles, so do the number of clingers. The nymphs' flat shape makes them perfectly adapted to fast-water habitats— turbulent currents slide easily over them without washing them off the bottom.

Nymphs are poor swimmers, but because they hang on to the bottom so well, they are rarely found drifting in the current. When it's time to emerge, however, the nymphs release their hold on the bottom and feebly swim to the surface. Duns of most species emerge in the surface film, although some species emerge underwater. Many traditional wet flies may owe their effectiveness to this underwater emergence behavior. Duns often provide exciting dry fly action during a hatch. Spinner falls of clingers sometimes produce fast fishing on summer evenings just at dusk.

Major Hatches of Clingers

Name	Emergence	Size	Dist.
Gordon Quill *Epeorus pleuralis*	Apr-May	N: 9-10mm A: 9-10mm	E
Yellow Quill *Epeorus* sp.	Jun-Aug	N: 8-15mm A: 8-15mm	E C W
Light Cahill or Pale Evening Dun *Heptagenia* sp.	Jun-Aug	N: 6-12mm A: 7-15mm	C W
Western March Brown *Rhithrogena morrisoni*	Mar-May	N: 8-12mm A: 8-12mm	W
American March Brown *Stenonema vicarium*	May-Jun	N: 10-14mm A: 12-15mm	E

Major Patterns and Tactics for Clingers

Stage	Patterns	Ref.	Tactic
Nymph	Gold-Ribbed Hare's Ear	2, 8	1
	March Brown	2, 8	
	Quill Gordon	2, 8	
Emerger	Hare's Ear Wet Fly	8	4 or 5
	Pheasant Tail Soft Hackle	2	
	Quill Gordon Wet Fly	2	
Dun	Light Cahill	2, 8	6
	Compara-Dun	2	
	Quill Gordon	2, 8	
	March Brown	8	
Spinner	Compara-Spinner	2	6 or 7

(Note: See p. 28 for information on references and p. 32 for information on tactics.)

Burrowers

Major families and genera of burrowers:

Families	Genera (# of species)
Ephemeridae	*Ephemera* (7)
	Hexagenia (5)
Polymitarcyidae	*Ephoron* (2)

Burrowers are the largest mayflies of North America. Nymphs are easily recognized by their tusk-like mandibles, large digging forelegs, large feather-like gills, and three tails heavily fringed with fine hairs. Adults are given away by their size and large hind wings. Two or three tails may be present depending on the genus; *Ephemera* have three tails, *Hexagenia* two. For species of *Ephoron*, the number of tails vary by sex; males have two tails, females three.

Burrowers may be abundant in both lake or stream habitats, but the nymphs require a soft sandy/gravel bottom (*Ephemera*) or a thick, muddy substrate (*Hexagenia*) to thrive. This type of habitat is uninhabitable to most other mayflies. Nymphs dig U-shaped burrows into the substrate where they spend the daylight hours, coming out to feed at night. To maintain a flow of fresh water through their tunnels, nymphs wave their gills to create a current. Burrowers are able to withstand oxygen levels too low for other mayflies to survive.

Burrower nymphs are good swimmers but are not inclined to do so until they are ready to emerge. At that time, the nymphs leave their burrows and swim to the surface where the adults emerge in the surface film. Large nymphs twitched to the surface are deadly during a hatch. Duns and spinners likewise become targets for fish, and their imitations will work well during the latter part of a hatch. Because most burrowers emerge at dusk, the best dry-fly fishing generally occurs after dark.

While restricted to areas with suitable habitat, the abundance and size of the burrowers can result in some of the most spectacular fishing of the season.

Major Hatches of Burrowers

Name	Emergence	Size	Dist.
Eastern Green Drake Ephemeridae *Ephemera guttulata*	Jun-Jul	N: 17-20mm A: 17-22mm	E
Brown Drake Ephemeridae *Ephemera simulans*	Jun-Aug	N: 12-20mm A: 15-20mm	C W
Big Yellow May Ephemeridae *Hexagenia limbata*	May-Aug	N: 18-35mm A: 22-35mm	E C W
White Mayfly Polymitarcyidae *Ephoron* sp.	Jul-Sep	N: 12-17mm A: 12-17mm	E C W

Major Patterns and Tactics for Burrowers

Stage	Patterns	Ref.	Tactics
Nymph	Big Yellow May	8	2 or 3
	Brown Drake	11	
Emerger	Same as above		3 or 5
Dun	Big Yellow May	11	6
	Brown Drake	8	
Spinner	Big Yellow May Spinner	11	6 or 7
	Compara-Spinner	2	

(Note: See p. 28 for information on references and p. 32 for information on tactics.)

References

The following books are devoted to mayflies or have chapters or sections of interest to those seeking more information on mayflies. That some are technical in nature should be obvious from their titles and publishers.

Arbona, Fred, Jr. *Mayflies, the Angler, and the Trout*. Tulsa, Oklahoma: Winchester Press, 1980.

Caucci and Nastasi. *Hatches*. Woodside, New York: Comparahatch, 1975.

Edmunds, George, Jr., Steven Jensen, and L. Berner. *The Mayflies of North and Central America*. Minneapolis: University of Minnesota Press, 1976.

Hubbard, M. D., and W. L. Peters. *Environmental Requirements and Pollution Tolerance of Ephemeroptera*. Cincinnati, Ohio: Environ. Monit. Sup. Lab, Off. Res. Dev. U.S.E.P.A, 1978.

Needham, J. G., J. R. Traver, and Y-C Hsu. *The Biology of Mayflies*. Ithaca, New York: Comstock, 1935. (Reprint: 1972, E. W. Classey Ltd., London.)

6. Stoneflies: Order Plecoptera

Key to Stonefly Nymphs, p. 79
Key to Stonefly Adults, p. 83

Stoneflies are an important part of insect life in streams throughout the country. However, with a few exceptions, such as Montana's "salmonfly" hatch, they don't provide flyfishers the excitement generated by mayfly or caddisfly hatches. This is partly due to their behavior— stoneflies don't show themselves readily as nymphs or adults. Adults prefer hiding on streamside foliage to flying, and nymphs seek crevices and cracks between bottom rocks and debris.

Still, it's easy to underestimate the importance of stoneflies. This is a common mistake, and many fishermen are caught unprepared when fish are feeding on them. This chapter will allow you to identify stoneflies and separate them into five basic groups. Suitable patterns and tactics to match them are also given.

Basic Identification and Similar Orders

The major characteristics of stonefly adults and nymphs are described in the keys. As nymphs, stoneflies are most often confused with mayfly nymphs. Adult stoneflies, on the other hand, are commonly confused with adult caddisflies and dobsonflies (Order Megaloptera). The following table will help separate these orders.

Nymphs

Identifying Characters	Stoneflies	Mayflies
Wing Pads	4, visible on mature nymphs	4 present but only 2 visible
Gills	Filamentous gills on thorax, head or abdomen, or gills absent	Plate-like gills on abdomen
Tails	2 approx. body length	3, sometimes 2 long tails
Claws	2 on each leg	1 on each leg

Adults

Identifying Characters	Stoneflies	Caddisflies	Dobsonflies
Wings	4, lie flat on top of abdomen	4, held tent-shaped over abdomen	4, lie flat on top of abdomen
Tails	2 ranging from very short to body length	None	None
Fine Hairs on Wings	None	Present	None

Size Range

Few other orders of aquatic insects show as large a range of size as stoneflies. Nymphs and adults of the largest species can be over 50mm (2") long, while the smallest species may only be 6mm (1/4"). Imitations must, therefore, be carefully selected to match the size of the natural, and a wide range of pattern sizes is necessary. Hook sizes ranging from #18 to #4 4XL may be required. The most common sizes range from #10 1XL to #6 3XL.

Life Cycle

Stoneflies, like mayflies, have incomplete metamorphosis. The amount of time spent in the egg, nymph, and adult stages varies widely with species. The smaller stoneflies generally have a one-year life cycle, but the large species may take two, three, or even four years to complete one generation.

Stage	Average Duration	Extremes
Egg	2-4 weeks	Several minutes (some Capniidae) to 2-4 months (most Perlidae)
Nymph	7-11 months	2-4 years (many Pteronarcidae and Perlidae)
Adult	1-3 weeks	2 or 3 days to several months

The majority of the life cycle is spent in the nymphal stage, making the nymph the stage most frequently eaten by fish. Nymphs remain abundant and available even after the adults have emerged, since younger year classes of nymphs are still in the stream. Temperature and the amount of suitable food have the greatest effect on the speed of nymphal development. Studies have shown water temperatures of 45-55 degrees F ideal for the development of many stoneflies.

During emergence to adults, the nymphs crawl out of the water onto the bank. Nymphs become more available to fish as they migrate to the banks, but adults are not generally available at the time of emergence. Because of the movement of the nymphs, fish are attracted to the water near the banks during stonefly emergence.

Adults mate on the ground instead of in flight. After mating, females fly to the water and, most often, release clusters of eggs as their abdomen touches the water's surface. Some species release their eggs above the water's surface, and others crawl underwater to deposit their eggs. It's during egg laying that adults are most available to the fish and when adult patterns are most effective. Adult stonefly activity is generally heaviest from afternoon to dusk.

North American Distribution and Abundance

Region	# of Families	# of Genera
East	9	50
Central	5	20
West	9	64
Total in N.A.	9	92

Approximate number of North American species: 500

Habitat Preferences

Stoneflies are inhabitants of flowing waters. Their greatest diversity occurs in cool mountain streams or spring waters. This preference for cool streams is reflected in the distribution chart, where the West, with its extensive mountain ranges, contains the greatest number of stonefly genera. The West is also where stoneflies are best known for their excellent hatches.

A few stoneflies do live in lakes. (One species is known to live in Lake Tahoe at depths of up to 200 feet.) These species are mostly restricted to high mountain lakes that maintain cold, well-oxygenated water.

The narrow range of habitats where stoneflies are found is partly due to their primitive gill structure. (As mentioned, some species lack gills entirely.) Their gill structure forces them to live where waters remain cold and well-oxygenated. Stream bottoms of large gravel and rubble are ideal for most stoneflies. These are the areas where you should concentrate your fishing with stonefly patterns.

Identification

The many species of stoneflies exhibit few differences in behavior. They are all primarily crawlers as nymphs. They swim poorly, and when washed into the current they drift near the bottom until they can find a new foothold. Nearly all emerge by crawling out on the bank, and the adults mate on streamside foliage.

Because of similar behavior patterns, the following keys divide the order into five groups based on size and color differences. This breakdown can greatly simplify your pattern selection for nymphs and adults.

Key to Stonefly Nymphs

Identification begins with inspection of the nymph for the type and location of its gills. Immature specimens may not have gills fully developed, making identification difficult. A hand lens may be needed to distinguish some of the characteristics described here.

1a. If gills appear as simple finger-like filaments near base of legs or along underside of head, or if gills are absent, go to **2**.

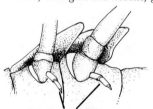

Finger-like gills

1b. If thickly branched gills are present at the base of legs and/or under thorax, go to **5**.

Thickly branched gills

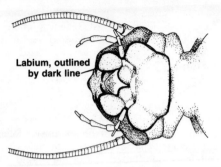

2a. If lower lip (labium) has 3 notches along outer margin (observe with hand lens), and body (excluding tails) is generally small, 6-12mm (1/4"-1/2"), go to **3**.

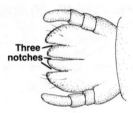

2b. If labium has single center notch, and body is small to moderate in size 6-22mm (1/4"-7/8"), go to **4**.

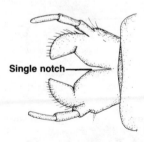

3a. If head has 2 dorsal eye spots (ocelli), and body shape is roach-like, it is a LITTLE YELLOW STONEFLY. Go to p. 89.

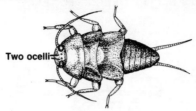

3b. If the head has 3 ocelli, and body shape is not roach-like, and if body color is uniformly brown to black, it is a LITTLE BROWN STONEFLY. Go to p. 87.

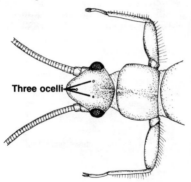

4a. If hind wing pads of mature nymph diverge from sides of body, and tails are as long as or longer than abdomen; and if body is often colored in a distinct pattern, it is a LITTLE YELLOW STONEFLY. Go to p. 89.

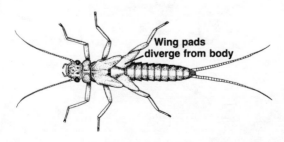

4b. If hind wing pads of mature nymph are parallel with body, and tails are shorter than abdomen; and if body is a uniform brown or green, it is a **LITTLE GREEN STONEFLY**. Go to p. 91.

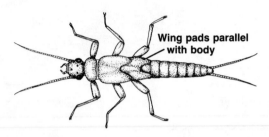

Wing pads parallel with body

5a. If branched gills are present on thorax and underside of first 2 or 3 abdominal segments, it is a **GIANT STONEFLY**. Go to p. 94.

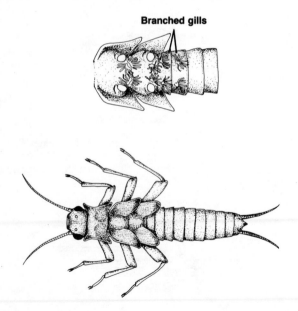

Branched gills

5b. If branched gills are present only on sides of thorax, never on abdominal segments, it is a GOLDEN STONEFLY. Go to p. 92.

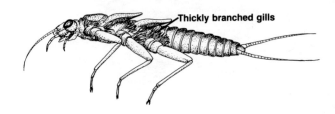

Thickly branched gills

Key to Stonefly Adults

Stonefly adults possess remnants of the gills found on nymphs. These remnant gills or the lack of them begin the identification process. A hand lens may be needed to distinguish some of the characteristics described here.

1a. If gill remnants are absent, or if present, are simple, finger-like gill remnants, not branched, go to **2**.

1b. If gill remnants on side of thorax and/or under abdomen appear thick and branched, go to **5**.

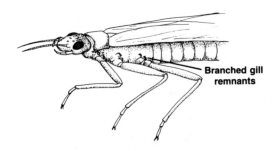

Branched gill remnants

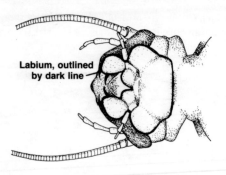

2a. If lower lip (labium) has 3 notches along outer margin (observe with hand lens), and the body (excluding tails) is generally small, 6-12mm (1/4"-1/2"), go to **3**.

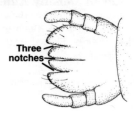

2b. If labium has a single center notch, and body color is brown, green, or yellow, uniformly colored or with distinct color markings, go to **4**.

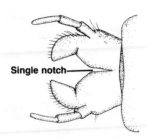

3a. If head has 2 dorsal eye spots (ocelli), and body shape is roach-like, it is a LITTLE YELLOW STONEFLY. Go to p. 89.

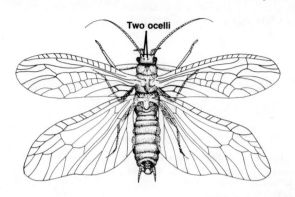

Two ocelli

3b. If head has 3 ocelli, and body is not roach-like; and if body color is uniform brown to black, it is a LITTLE BROWN STONEFLY. Go to p. 87.

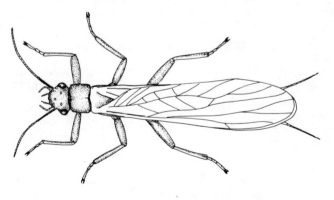

4a. If anal cell of fore wing shows two branches (veins) leaving cell separately, and body color is shades of brown or yellow; and if body (excluding tails) is 6-22mm (1/4"-7/8"), it is a LITTLE YELLOW STONEFLY. Go to p. 89.

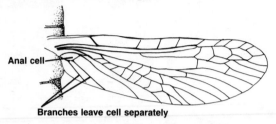

Anal cell

Branches leave cell separately

4b. If anal cell of fore wing shows a single forked or unforked vein leaving cell, and body color is shades of green or yellow; and if body is 10-13mm (3/8"-1/2"), it is a LITTLE GREEN STONEFLY. Go to p. 91.

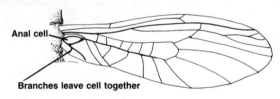

Anal cell

Branches leave cell together

5a. If branched gill remnants are present on undersides of first two or three abdominal segments, it is a GIANT STONEFLY. Go to p. 94.

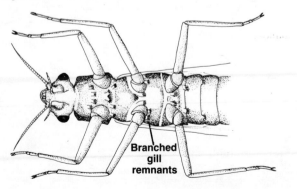

Branched gill remnants

5b. If branched gill remnants are present on sides of thorax but not on abdominal segments, it is a GOLDEN STONEFLY. Go to p. 92.

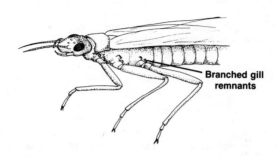

**Branched gill
remnants**

Little Brown Stoneflies

Major families and genera of Little Brown Stoneflies:

Families	Genera (# of species)
Nemouridae	*Nemoura* (4)
	Amphinemura (13)
	Podmosta (5)
	Soyedina (8)
Taeniopterygidae	*Taeniopteryx* (10)
	Strophopteryx (7)
	Taenionema (8)
Leuctridae	*Leuctra* (20)
	Paraleuctra (8)
	Megaleuctra (5)
Capniidae	*Allocapnia* (39)
	Capnia (50)

Little Brown Stoneflies are small, less than 12mm (1/2") long and are a uniform brown to black color. Nymphs lack gills or have only a few finger-like filaments positioned under the head. Many species have numerous long hairs on their legs and body that trap silt and debris and provide a natural camouflage. A definitive characteristic of both nymphs and adults is the three shallow notches along the outer margin of the labium. A small hand lens is usually sufficient to see them.

Little Brown Stoneflies are a major component of mountain streams, and often make up the majority of stonefly species. They also occur in larger rivers where the substrate is smaller and temperatures are warmer. Their great diversity (260+ species) makes it difficult to identify them even to the family level. The Capniidae can be easily recognized in the adult stage, since it's the only family of Little Brown Stoneflies with long tails as an adult. The wings of Leuctridae typically roll closely around the abdomen giving them a very narrow "needle-like" appearance.

The importance of Little Brown Stoneflies is often overlooked by flyfishers, primarily because of the insect's small size and the time of year it emerges. The best hatches occur in the winter or early spring when most fishermen are at home tying flies or working hard enough to afford summer vacations. But if you're able to venture streamside during January, February, or March, you'll likely find Little Brown Stonefly adults as one of the only insects present in good numbers. Fishing a small dry fly along the banks or through pockets and runs can provide considerable sport. Some Little Brown Stoneflies will still be present during the spring and summer, but by then other hatches have reached peak activity thereby diminishing the stonefly's importance.

Major Hatches of Little Brown Stoneflies

Name	Emergence	Size	Dist.
Winter Stonefly Capniidae *Capnia* sp.	Nov-Feb	N: 6-10mm A: 7-10mm	E W
Needle Fly Leuctridae *Leuctra* sp.	Aug-Nov	N: 7-12mm A: 9-12mm	E C W
Early Brown Stones Nemouridae *Nemoura* and *Zapada*	Jan-May	N: 7-12mm A: 9-12mm	E C W
Little Red Stones or February Red Taeniopterygidae *Taeniopteryx* and *Taenionema*	Jan-Apr	N: 7-12mm A: 9-12mm	E W

Major Patterns and Tactics for Little Brown Stoneflies

Stage	Patterns	Ref.	Tactics
Nymph	Little Brown Stone	11	1
	Early Black Stone	2	
Adult	Little Brown Stone Dry	11	6 or 7
	Brown Elk Hair Caddis	2, 8	

(Note: See p. 28 for information on references and p. 32 for information on tactics.)

Little Yellow Stoneflies

Major families and genera of Little Yellow Stoneflies:

Families	Genera (# of species)
Perlodidae	*Isoperla* (50)
	Cultus (4)
	Duira (3)
	Isogenoides (9)
	Megarcys (5)
Peltoperlidae	*Tallaperla* (6)
	Yoroperla (2)

These two families of Little Yellow Stoneflies differ in shape, but as adults they are both yellowish brown in color and are, therefore, included together. Peltoperlids have a distinctive roach-like shape and only two ocelli. Of the two families, they are the least common, but they can be locally abundant.

Species of Perlodidae are the typical Little Yellow Stonefly. Nymphs are yellow to light brown with very distinctive dark stripes or irregular markings on the abdomen and thorax. Gills are frequently absent or form simple, finger-like filaments if present. Adults range in color from bright yellow to a brownish orange. All have two easily-seen tails, and the front wings have two separate veins leaving the anal cell (see Key to Stonefly Adults).

Approximately 120 species of Little Yellow Stoneflies occur across the country. The greatest abundance is found in the East and in the mountain areas of the West. Gravel or rocky riffle areas provide the best habitat for most species, although the peltoperlids seem to prefer spring creeks where moss beds or plant debris cover the bottom. Streams must remain cool and well-oxygenated all year for really good populations of Little Yellow Stoneflies to occur.

Nymphs mature in less than a year. Their greatest abundance and availability occurs during their annual migration to shore prior to emergence. Nymphs of peltoperlids are plant feeders, while many perlodids are predators feeding on smaller aquatic insects. Both are common in stream drift, and nymph imitations often prove effective. While most nymphs swim poorly, some of the larger perlodids (e.g. *Megarcys* sp.) move effectively through the water with a snake-like swimming motion.

A few Little Yellow Stoneflies emerge in spring, but most hatches occur in summer. Look for the females on warm summer evenings when they frequently form large swarms over riffles and runs to lay their eggs. As they gently glide to the water's surface, trout wait below, eager to intercept them.

Major Hatches of Little Yellow Stoneflies

Name	Emergence	Size	Dist.
Yellow Sally	Jul-Sep	N: 7-16mm	E C W
Perlodidae *Isoperla* sp.		A: 7-16mm	
Early Orange Stone	Apr-Jun	N: 13-22mm	E W
Perlodidae		A: 13-22mm	
Isogenoides and *Megarcys*			
Summer Stone	May-Aug	N: 6-12mm	E W
Peltoperlidae		A: 6-12mm	

Major Patterns and Tactics for Little Yellow Stoneflies

Stage	Patterns	Ref.	Tactics
Nymph	Little Yellow Stone	11	1
	Stonefly Creeper	2, 8	
Adult	Little Yellow Stone Dry	2, 11	6 or 7
	Light Caddis	2	

(Note: See p. 28 for information on references and p. 32 for information on tactics.)

Little Green Stoneflies

Major families and genera of Little Green Stoneflies:

Families	Genera (# of species)
Chloroperlidae	*Alloperla* (21)
	Sweltsa (23)

Little Green Stoneflies closely resemble Little Yellow Stoneflies. Nymphs of Little Green Stoneflies are a uniform green or brown color, with brown being most common. They lack the distinct markings of Little Yellow Stonefly nymphs. Gills are absent from all Little Green Stoneflies, and their tails are short. Adults vary in color from bright green to pale yellow. The yellow species so closely resemble Little Yellow Stoneflies, that the only way tell them apart positively is by checking the differences in wing venation described in the Key to Stonefly Adults.

Little Green Stoneflies are not common in the central part of the country but can be abundant in the eastern and western sections. Again, cool mountain streams provide the best habitat. Riffle areas with moderate to slow currents where plant debris collects is the ideal habitat for many species. Adults are found on streamside foliage.

Nymphs are primarily predators. They crawl among plant debris and rocks looking for small insect larva. They generally are not as common in the drift as many of the Little Yellow Stoneflies, and their importance varies widely between streams. Nymphs mature in less than a year. Mature nymphs migrate to shore where they crawl out on rocks or sticks just above the water line to emerge. The complete life cycle requires about one year.

While the nymphs generally go unnoticed, the adults become quite obvious on summer evenings when females form large swarms over the water to lay their eggs. Their behavior is similar to the Little Yellow Stoneflies; the gravid females glide gently down to the water's surface releasing small clusters of eggs as their abdomen touches. This activity provides the best fishing opportunities. Small dry flies fished dead drift in riffles or runs can be quite productive when females swarm to lay eggs.

Major Hatches of Little Green Stoneflies

Name	Emergence	Size	Dist.
Little Green Stone	Jul-Aug	N: 7-12mm	E W
Chloroperlidae		A: 10-12mm	
Alloperla and *Sweltsa*			

Major Patterns and Tactics for Little Green Stoneflies

Stage	Patterns	Ref.	Tactics
Nymph	Little Brown Stone	11	1
	Pheasant Tail Nymph	2, 8	
Adult	Little Green Stone	8	6 or 7
	Little Yellow Stone	2, 11	
	Partridge and Green Soft Hackle	2	

(Note: See p. 28 for information on references and p. 32 for information on tactics.)

Golden Stoneflies

Major families and genera of Golden Stoneflies:

Families	Genera (# of species)
Perlidae	*Acroneuria* (11)
	Calineuria (1)
	Hesperoperla (1)
	Perlesta (2)
	Doroneuria (2)

All Golden Stoneflies belong to the same family, but there are numerous genera and species. They are large stoneflies, reaching lengths of 25-50mm (1"-2"). Nymphs have distinctive dark markings on the thoracic segments and gill tufts at the base of each leg. They range in color from pale yellowish tan to dark brown. Adults are similar in size to the nymphs. Many are a rich golden brown color, which gives this group its name. Other species are a dark brown color. To confirm identification of adults, look for nymphal gill remnants at the base of the legs.

Golden Stoneflies are distributed across the country, but the best hatches occur in the West, from the Rocky Mountains to the Pacific Coast, where two species, *Calineuria californica* and *Hesperoperla pacifica*, predominate. Good populations occur in both small streams and large rivers. Riffles with a rocky substrate provide the best habitat. Golden Stoneflies are the most widespread and abundant of the large stoneflies.

Golden Stone nymphs are predators. As such, they actively crawl over the bottom in search of prey, primarily smaller aquatic insects. This active behavior frequently causes nymphs to get washed into the current and drift along the bottom. Nymph imitations are consistent producers on streams where Golden Stoneflies are abundant. Nymphs require two to three years to mature fully. Mature nymphs migrate to the banks and crawl out prior to adult emergence. Large migrations of nymphs can produce exceptional nymph fishing.

Adult Golden Stoneflies congregate on streamside foliage where they mate. Adults tend to be clumsy fliers and during heavy hatches they fall into the water throughout the day. Females fly to the water's surface in the afternoon and evening laden with eggs, creating the best fishing opportunities with dry flies.

Major Hatches of Golden Stoneflies

Name	Emergence	Size	Dist.
Golden Stone *Calineuria* *californica*	Jun-Aug	N: 24-38mm A: 25-38mm	W
Brown Willow Fly *Acroneuria* and *Hesperoperla*	May-Aug	N: 22-35mm A: 22-35mm	E C W
Great Stonefly *Perlesta*	Jul-Aug	N: 25-38mm A: 25-38mm	E C

Major Patterns and Tactics for Golden Stoneflies

Stage	Patterns	Ref.	Tactics
Nymph	Golden Stone	8	1 or 2
	Bitch Creek	2	
	Kaufmann's Golden Stone	2, 3	
Adult	Golden Stone Dry	2	6 or 7
	Stimulator	2	

(Note: See p. 28 for information on references and p. 32 for information on tactics.)

Giant Stoneflies

Major families and genera of Giant Stoneflies:

Families	Genera (# of species)
Pteronarcidae	*Pteronarcys* (8)
	Pteronarcella (2)

Giant stoneflys live up to their name by being the largest stoneflies in North America. Nymphs of 50mm (2") in length are common, and lengths up to 75mm (3") can be reached. Nymphs are easily recognized by their large size, uniform dark brown to black color, and gill tufts extending to the underside of the first two or three abdominal segments. They also have a rounder body and shorter tails than most other stoneflies.

With a total wingspan of over three inches, the adults look even more impressive than the nymphs. Adults generally appear dark brown or black in color, but inspection of the underside of the body reveals colors ranging from reddish-orange to pale tan. Make sure you take this color into account when tying or selecting patterns to imitate them.

Big rivers, big flies, and big fish are as western as buffalo chips and beef jerky. The abundance of Giant Stoneflies in western streams is a major factor contributing to the big flies/big fish notion. The salmonfly hatch (*Pteronarcys californica*) on rivers like the Big Hole and Madison are legendary and attract flyfishers from around the world. Giant Stoneflies also occur in the Midwest and East. The most important species there is *Pteronarcys dorsata*. Wherever Giant Stoneflies are found they provide a constant food supply for fish.

Giant Stonefly nymphs feed on plant debris or rooted vegetation. Areas with moderate currents and a rocky bottom that traps plant debris provide excellent habitat. Species of *Pteronarcys* tend to be most common in moderate- to large-sized rivers, while *Pteronarcella* species are more common in small streams and creeks. More than one species may occur in the same section of stream.

Nymphs require two to four years to fully mature. During their development they are regularly eaten by fish, and patterns that imitate them provide good nymph fishing year round on streams with large populations. At maturity nymphs migrate to the banks where they crawl out, and the adults emerge. These migrations can be very heavy and can provide exceptional nymph fishing.

Adult emergence typically occurs during the night or early morning.

Adults spend most of their time on streamside foliage. During heavy hatches, the banks are nearly covered with adults. A steady supply of adults is available for fish on these days. After mating on the foliage, females fly back to the water and lay their eggs by touching the water's surface or by releasing clusters of eggs above the water. Dry-fly fishing can be spectacular at such times, as the largest fish joyfully race for each oversized mouthful.

Major Hatches of Giant Stoneflies

Name	Emergence	Size	Dist.
Giant Salmon Fly *Pteronarcys californica*	Apr-Jul	N: 25-50mm A: 30-50mm	W
Giant Black Stonefly *Pteronarcys dorsata*	May-Aug	N: 35-55mm A: 35-55mm	E C W
Small Salmon Fly *Pteronarcella badia*	May-Jul	N: 25-40mm A: 25-40mm	W

Major Patterns and Tactics for Giant Stoneflies

Stage	Patterns	Ref.	Tactics
Nymph	Large Dark Stone	8	1 or 2
	Box Canyon Stone	2, 8	
	Dark Stone Nymph	11	
	Montana Stone	7	
Adult	Dark Stone Dry	2	6 or 7
	Sofa Pillow	2, 8	
	Bird's Stonefly	2	
	Troth Salmonfly	2	

(Note: See p. 28 for information on references and p. 32 for information on tactics.)

References

All but two of the books listed here are technical works. Although all of them provide useful information, you may wish to begin your research with the books written for flyfishermen, *Stoneflies* and *Stoneflies for the Angler*.

Bauman, R.W., Arden R. Gaufin, and Rebecca Surdick. *The Stoneflies (Plecoptera) of the Rocky Mountains*. American Entomological Society, 1977.

Frison, T. H. *The Stoneflies (Plecoptera) of Illinois*. Illinois: Bulletin Illinois Nat. Hist. Surv. 20, 1935. (Reprint: 1975, Entomol. Rep. Specialists, Los Angeles.)

Hitchcock, S. W. *The Plecoptera or Stoneflies of Connecticut*. Connecticut: Bulletin St. Geol. Nat. Hist. Surv. Conn. 107, 1974.

Jewett, Stanley, Jr. *The Stoneflies (Plecoptera) of the Pacific Northwest*. Corvallis, Oregon: Oregon State University Press, 1959.

Leiser, Eric and Robert H. Boyle. *Stoneflies for the Angler*. New York: Alfred A. Knopf, 1982.

Richards, Carl, Doug Swisher, and Fred Arbona, Jr. *Stoneflies*. New York: Nick Lyons Books/Winchester Press, 1980.

Surdick, R. F., and A. R. Gaufin. *Environmental Requirements and Pollution Tolerance of Plecoptera*. Cincinnati, Ohio: Environmental Monit. Sup. Lab., Off. Res. Dev. U.S.E.P.A., 1978.

7. Dragonflies and Damselflies: Order Odonata

Key to Odonata Nymphs, p. 102
Key to Odonata Adults, p. 105

Dragonflies and damselflies are the summer companions of every school boy lucky enough to hunt the banks of creeks and ponds. Their large size, bright colors, and aerial ability have made them frequent subjects of naturalists and poets . . . and of old wives' tales. A part of local folklore across the country, dragonflies and damselflies have been given common names such as "Biddies," "Clubtails," and "Snake Darners."

While Odonata adults may be well known to everyone, the nymphs tend to remain a mystery, hidden in their underwater haven. For the flyfisher, however, the nymphs are the most important stage to imitate. Slow rivers, sloughs, and lakes are the favorite haunts of most Odonata nymphs.

The order Odonata is divided into two suborders: Anisoptera (dragonflies) and Zygoptera (damselflies). Dragonflies and damselflies, although closely related, look distinctly different. Damselflies, for instance, are more slender and delicate in appearance than dragonflies and, at rest, hold their wings over the abdomen, instead of outstretched.

The keys in this chapter divide the order into four important groups based on behavior. Information important to the imitation of each group follows the keys.

Basic Identification and Similar Orders

Identification of dragonflies and damselflies is relatively easy. Adults have four large wings held back over the abdomen (damselflies) or outstreched to the sides (dragonflies), a long slender abdomen, and no tails. Dragonfly adults are particularly superb fliers, and their aerial skills make for quick identification.

Nymphs are likewise distinct in shape and behavior. All have an arm-like lower lip, or labium, that can be thrust out like the hinged tongue of a frog to capture prey. Eyes are large, for hunting, and dragonfly nymphs have a unique method of swimming which was aptly described this way by Jean Henri Fabre, a famous 19th century French naturalist: ". . . it fills its hinder parts, a yawning funnel, with water, spirts it out again and advances just so far as the recoil of its water cannon."

In appearance, Odonata nymphs might be confused with hellgrammites, alderflies, or mayflies. Adults resemble some hellgrammite adults (dobsonflies) and some Neuroptera, an order of terrestrial insects commonly called lacewings and antlions. The table below will help differentiate these insects.

| | | Nymphs | | |
	Odonata	Alderflies	Hellgram-mites	Mayflies
Gills	Internal or 3 tail-like plates	Lateral abdominal filaments	Lateral abdominal filaments	Plate-like gills on abdomen
Tails	None (gills sometimes look like tails)	Single long gill filament	None	3, some-times 2
Wing Pads	4	0	0	4, but only 2 distinct
Claws Per Leg	2	2	2	1

| | | Adults | |
	Odonata	Hellgram-mites	Lacewings/Antlions
Wings	4 large wings held above abdomen or outstretched at sides	4, large and held tent-like over abdomen	4, large and held tent-like over abdomen
Antennae	Short, bristle-like	Long, ½ body length	Long, ½ body length
Legs	With many long spines and hairs	Hairs or spines sparse	Hairs or spines sparse

Size Range

Dragonflies and damselflies are medium- to large-sized insects. Dragonflies tend to be slightly larger than damselflies, but either makes a good mouthful for a fish. Mature nymphs range from 15-50mm (3/4"-2") and can be imitated with hook sizes of #10 3XL to #4 3XL. Adults are even larger than nymphs. Body length may range from 30-100mm (1 1/4"-4") and their wingspan may be from 25-100mm (1"-4"). Because of their long bodies, most patterns are tied with extended bodies. Hook sizes from #10 to #6 3XL may be needed.

Life Cycle

Odonata have incomplete metamorphosis. Because this order is distributed from the Tropics to the Arctic, there's a wide variation in life cycles. In most cases, damselflies complete development in one year, with two generations a year not uncommon. Dragonflies typically require two years and often longer to complete one generation. Studies have found that abundance of food, water temperature, and photoperiod all play a role in the nymph's development and the timing of emergence.

Stage	Average Duration	Extremes
Egg	2-4 weeks	3-5 days to 3-6 months
Nymph	10-11 months or 18-24 months	2-3 months to 5-6 years
Adult	4-6 weeks	1-2 weeks to 3 months

As with other aquatic insects, the nymph is the most available stage of Odonata, and it is the nymph that is more important than the adult as a food source for fish. Nymphs are available to fish for a longer period, and adults, especially dragonflies, are such good fliers that fish can rarely catch them. The one-year life cycle of most damselflies results in the greatest abundance of nymphs in the late spring or early summer, just before emergence. Since dragonfly nymphs generally require more than one year to mature, they remain available to fish year round.

The availability of nymphs (and therefore their importance to fish and to flyfishermen) is also enhanced by their behavior. All Odonata nymphs are predators, and most actively hunt their prey by climbing through aquatic plants or debris. This activity exposes them to fish. The jet-propelled swimming behavior of many dragonflies also increases their exposure.

While fish feed on nymphs throughout the year, the heaviest

feeding occurs when the nymphs migrate to shore prior to adult emergence. Damselfly migrations can be very concentrated. This fact, coupled with their slow, open-water swimming behavior during migration, produces ideal fishing conditions. Dragonfly nymphs migrate along the bottom rather than swimming in open water, but fish still feed on them eagerly. Their imitations can be very productive when fished near shore.

Adult emergence occurs on shoreline grasses or trees. As a result, adults are not available to fish during emergence, but frogs, birds, and other predators hunt them out. This is an extremely vulnerable time, since most Odonata take one to two hours to escape the nymphal shuck, harden their wings, and fly away. To avoid predators, most species of dragonflies emerge at night; most damselflies emerge during early- to mid-morning.

Unlike most adult aquatic insects, Odonata adults feed actively. The adults' spiny legs form an effective basket in which the prey is caught. (Indeed, one of the authors had a Firehole River dragonfly capture his Elk Hair Caddis in mid-air and start chewing on it; the dragonfly dropped the fly only after it felt pressure from the line being retrieved.) Mosquitoes make up a large part of their diet, and dragonflies have been used effectively to control mosquito populations without spraying. Adults often travel many miles from water to feed.

After feeding for one or two weeks, the adults begin mating and egg laying. Males become quite territorial during mating and readily fight other males. Mating typically occurs in the air, where males and females are often seen flying in tandem during copulation. It is during egg laying that fish get their best opportunity to feed on adults. The slower-flying damselflies seem to be particularly easy for fish to catch. On warm afternoons in June or July, large numbers of egg-laying damselflies are often eaten selectively by fish.

North American Distribution and Abundance

Region	# of Families	# of Genera
East	10	54
Central	8	46
West	11	61
Total in N.A.	11	88

Approximate number of North American species: 415

Habitat Preferences

Odonata are primarily inhabitants of slow rivers, sloughs, and lakes or ponds. The distribution chart shows the West with a slightly larger number of families and genera than the eastern or central states. This is due to the greater variety of habitats found in the West. However, Odonata reach their greatest abundance in the central and eastern states. The warm climates in the South and Southwest also have a rich fauna of dragonflies and damselflies.

While all 11 families contain some species that live in flowing water, Odonata are of greatest importance to fishermen in lakes and ponds. Areas with thick aquatic plants provide excellent cover and hunting areas for the nymphs. Tangles of wood and plant debris also provide suitable habitat for many species. Sandy banks are a marginal habitat, although rocky beaches are used by some dragonflies.

Adults are often selective about the egg-laying sites they use, which in turn affects the distribution of nymphs. Most adults lay their eggs on floating plants or underwater in the stems of plants. Specific species of plants or parts of the plant will often be used by different Odonata species as a depository for their eggs.

Identification

Separating damselflies from dragonflies is the first step in identification of Odonata. This is relatively simple for both nymphs and adults using the characters outlined in the following keys.

Damselflies are not subdivided into groups because of the consistency in behavior and general shape within their suborder. Similar patterns and tactics work for any of the damselflies. Only their size, color, and time of emergence varies.

Dragonfly nymphs, however, are subdivided into three groups: climbers, sprawlers, and burrowers. These groupings describe the nymph's behavior. Adult dragonflies are not keyed into these three groups, since they aren't readily taken by fish.

Key to Odonata Nymphs

This key begins by differentiating between damselflies and dragonflies.

1a. If abdomen ends in 3 tail-like flat gills, and body is slender with head wider than thorax and abdomen, it is a DAMSELFLY. Go to p. 106.

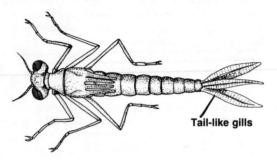

Tail-like gills

1b. If abdomen is missing tail-like gills, and body is stout with head usually narrower than thorax or abdomen, it is one of the DRAGONFLIES. Go to **2.**

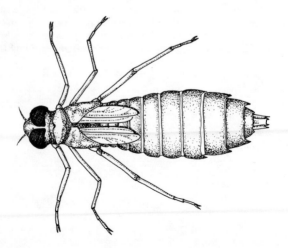

2a. If arm-like labium (lower lip) is flat, fitting almost completely under head when retracted, go to **3**.

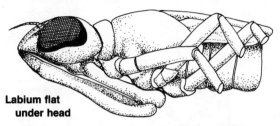

Labium flat under head

2b. If arm-like labium is spoon-shaped, partially covering front of head when retracted, go to **4**.

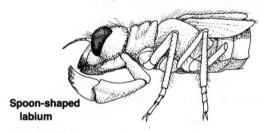

Spoon-shaped labium

3a. If antennae are 4-segmented, with third segment very large and fourth segment small, and body is typically round and squat, it is a BURROWER (Family: Gomphidae). Go to p. 107.

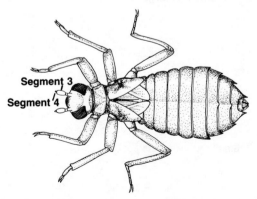

Segment 3
Segment 4

3b. If antennae have 6 or 7 segments, and body is generally long and slender, it is a CLIMBER. Go to p. 109.

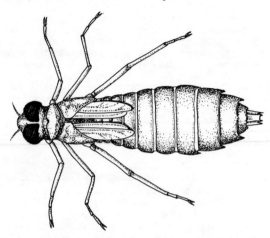

4a. If lateral lobes of labium have large, irregular, jagged teeth, it is a BURROWER. (Family: Cordulegastridae). Go to p. 107.

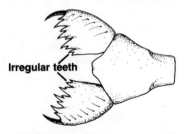

4b. If teeth on lateral lobes of labium are small, rounded, and evenly sized, it is a SPRAWLER. Go to p. 110.

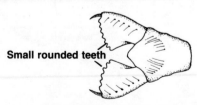

Key to Odonata Adults

This very simple key will help you decide whether the specimen you've collected is a damselfly or dragonfly.

1a. If front and hind wings are similar in size and shape, and wings are held parallel to body when at rest, it is a DAMSELFLY. Go to p. 106.

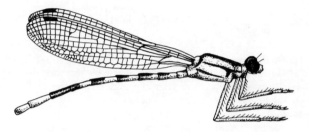

1b. If hind wings are much wider at base than front wings, and wings are held at right angle to body when at rest, it is a DRAGONFLY. Go to p. 107.

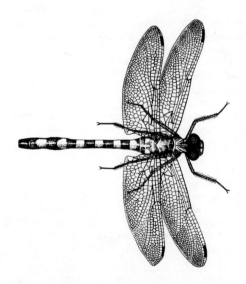

Damselflies

Major families and genera of damselflies:

Families	Genera (# of species)
Calopterygidae	*Calopteryx* (5)
Lestidae	*Archilestes* (2)
	Lestes (16)
Coenagrionidae	*Argia* (27)
	Enallagma (35)
	Ischnura (13)

Damselfly nymphs are easily identified by their three tail-like gills. Damselfly adults can be recognized by the way they hold their wings—straight back over the abdomen instead of out to each side. The eyes of damselflies are smaller and more widely separated than the eyes of dragonfly adults.

Damselfly nymphs occur in a wide variety of habitats. Of the families listed above, Calopterygidae and Lestidae frequently inhabit slow-moving sections of streams and rivers. The family Coenagrionidae is the most abundant group in lakes and ponds and is the largest family with over 90 known species. Most damselfly species prefer areas with abundant aquatic plants. This provides them room to hunt their prey and protects them from other predators such as dragonfly nymphs and fish.

Most damselflies are climbers—they climb along the stems and leaves of underwater plants looking for prey. They eat a wide variety of food, including mayflies, midges, freshwater shrimp, copepods, and smaller damselflies.

Nymphs mature in approximately one year. Fully mature nymphs become restless and migrate to shore, where they crawl out of the water to emerge. Large numbers of migrating damselflies often swim slowly toward shore during emergence. A damselfly nymph pattern retrieved slowly along weedbeds will often produce exceptional flyfishing at such times.

Adult damselflies are generally seen hanging on to the leaves of cattails or shrubs along the banks or flying out over the water searching for small insects to eat. It's also common to see them on the surface of the water when they're laying eggs or if a breeze blows them in. When large numbers become available, fish will feed on them selectively. This is the best time for an adult damselfly pattern.

Major Hatches of Damselflies

Name	Emergence	Size	Dist.
Bandwings or Ruby Spots Calopterygidae *Calopteryx*	May-Aug	N: 25-50mm A: 30-55mm	E C W
Marsh Spreadwings Lestidae *Lestes*	Apr-Aug	N: 20-30mm A: 30-45mm	E C W
Dancers Coenagrionidae *Argia*	Jun-Sep	N: 15-25mm A: 30-40mm	E C W
Bluets Coenagrionidae *Enallagma*	May-Sep	N: 20-30mm A: 25-40mm	E C W
Forktails Coenagrionidae *Ischnura*	Apr-Jul	N: 15-25mm A: 25-35mm	E C W

(Note: The life histories of damselflies vary widely across the country. The emergence dates given above are only meant as a guide. Emergence times may be different in southern or far northern states.)

Major Patterns and Tactics for Damselflies

Stage	Patterns	Ref.	Tactics
Nymph	Green Damsel Nymph	2, 8, 11	9 or 10
	Green Damsel	8	
	Fair Damsel	7, 8	
Adult	Elk Hair Damsel	7	8
	Green Damsel Wet	11	

(Note: See p. 28 for information on references and p. 32 for information on tactics.)

Dragonfly Burrowers

Major families and genera of dragonfly burrowers:

Families	Genera (# of species)
Cordulegastridae	*Cordulegaster* (8)
Gomphidae	*Gomphus* (14)
	Ophiogomphus (15)
	Stylurus (12)

Most dragonfly burrowers belong to the family Gomphidae. This is a large family with over 90 species in North America. Nymphs are slightly compressed dorso-ventrally giving them a broad, flat shape. Nymphs mature in approximately three years, reaching a length of 18-38mm (3/4"-1 1/2").

Adults are moderately-sized dragonflies, with their eyes widely separated on top of the head. They tend to be black, brown, or green in coloration, and they often have a club-like swelling on the end of the abdomen, hence the common name "clubtails."

Burrowers, as their name implies, prefer a life in the sediments. Rather than actively hunt their prey, they dig themselves into sand and silt and wait in ambush for an unsuspecting victim. While these nymphs can swim with jet-propelled squirts, they remain motionless or move very slowly unless disturbed. When mature, they crawl along the bottom until they reach the bank, where they climb out to emerge.

Imitations of burrowers should be broad and flat. To imitate the sedentary habits of the natural, a slow retrieve is necessary. Let the fly sink to the lake bottom, along the edges where debris has accumulated, or to the stream bottom in pools. A sinking line may be necessary. Retrieve the fly with a slow hand-twist retrieve.

Major Hatches of Burrowers

Name	Emergence	Size	Dist.
Biddies	May-Jul	N: 35-45mm	E W
Cordulegastridae		A: 70-80mm	
Cordulegaster			
Common Clubtails	May-Aug	N: 30-40mm	E C W
Gomphidae		A: 45-55mm	
Gomphus			
Snake Darners	May-Jul	N: 25-30mm	E C W
Gomphidae		A: 45-55mm	
Ophiogomphus			

Major Patterns and Tactics for Burrowers

Stage	Patterns	Ref.	Tactics
Nymph	Assam Dragon	7	9 or 10
	Carey Special	8	

(Note: See p. 28 for information on references and p. 32 for information on tactics.)

Dragonfly Climbers

Major families and genera of dragonfly climbers:

Families	**Genera (# of species)**
Aeshnidae	*Aeshna* (20)
	Anax (4)

Nearly all dragonfly climbers belong to the family Aeshnidae. This family contains almost 40 species in North America. Several other genera occur in specific regions of the United States, but the two listed above are the most abundant and widespread. The greatest diversity of Aeshnids occurs in the South and East. In the West, almost all species belong to the genus *Aeshna*.

Aeshnid nymphs have a long slender body in comparison to the burrowers and sprawlers. They're well adapted for climbing through aquatic plants in search of prey. They swim with jet-propelled squirts when moving through open water. Most nymphs require two to three years to reach maturity. Mature nymphs range from 25-50mm (1"-2") long. The nymph's color tends to match that of its surroundings. Browns, grays, and various shades of green are typical.

Adults are frequently seen on summer days along lakes and ponds as well as many miles from water. They are large and commonly have blue and black or green and black bodies. They are excellent fliers, which makes them difficult for fish or fishermen to catch.

Climbers are the largest, most active, and to the flyfisherman probably the most important group of dragonflies. Their importance is largely due to the active behavior of the nymphs. Rather than wait for their prey, climbers actively hunt it. Nymphs are abundant on downed logs and wood debris or on the stems and leaves of aquatic plants. Here they clamber along, constantly on the lookout for something to eat. Once prey is spotted, the climber nymph stalks it like a cat until it's close enough to thrust out its labium and grab the victim.

Climbers are also more likely than either the sprawlers or burrowers to swim through the water in jet-propelled bursts when disturbed. The climbers' active hunting and swimming behavior makes them more exposed and available to fish than the camouflaged sprawlers and burrowers.

Patterns to imitate climbers should match the slender shape of the naturals. Many good local patterns have been developed. Because the climbers are more active in the water, a strip retrieve is often effective. Cast into or along the edges of weedbeds with a sinking or sink-tip line and retrieve the fly with a series of two- to four-inch strips. It often helps to pause slightly between each strip. Experiment with fast and slow retrieves to determine which works better. These tactics are especially deadly when nymphs are migrating to shallows for emergence. Such migrations generally occur under darkness in the late evening or early morning.

Major Hatches of Climbers

Name	Emergence	Size	Dist.
Blue Darners	Apr-Sep	N: 35-50mm	E C W
Aeshnidae		A: 45-80mm	
Aeshna			
Green Darners	Apr-Sep	N:40-50mm	E C W
Aeshnidae		A: 70-85mm	
Anax			

Major Patterns and Tactics for Climbers

Stage	Patterns	Ref.	Tactics
Nymph	Beaverpelt	2, 8	9
	Randall's Green Dragon	2, 3	
	Peacock Dragon	7	
	Carey Special	8	

(Note: See p. 28 for information on references and p. 32 for information on tactics.)

Dragonfly Sprawlers

Major families and genera of dragonfly sprawlers:

Families	Genera (# of species)
Macromiidae	*Macromia* (8)
Corduliidae	*Neurocordulia* (6)
	Somatochlora (26)
Libellulidae	*Erythemis* (3)
	Leucorrhinia (7)
	Libellula (16)
	Sympetrum (13)

Dragonfly sprawlers are most commonly members of the family Libellulidae. This family is one of the most common and widespread groups of dragonflies in North America, with approximately 90 known species.

Sprawler nymphs are even more broad and squat than the burrowers. They have long, almost spider-like legs. Nymphs generally mature in two years and reach lengths of 18-30mm (3/4"-1 1/4"). Adults tend to be moderate- to small-sized dragonflies and are often brightly colored. Bright red *Sympetrum* adults, for example, make a colorful contrast to the green vegetation on which they are seen.

Sprawlers are most abundant and important in lakes. Like the burrowers, they wait for their prey rather than hunt it. The bodies of many of these nymphs are covered with long hairs and hooks, which effectively catch silt and pieces of debris providing excellent camouflage. Nymphs are particularly abundant on wood and plant debris and on the stems or around the bases of aquatic plants.

The same patterns and tactics described for the burrowers can be used to imitate the sprawlers. Because the nymphs tend to move slowly, a slow hand-twist retrieve right along the bottom best imitates the natural. These tactics can be very effective when used along the edges of weedbeds on cloudy overcast days or in the evening and early morning.

Major Hatches of Sprawlers

Name	Emergence	Size	Dist.
River Skimmers Macromiidae *Macromia*	Jun-Aug	N: 30-40mm A: 65-75mm	E W
Bog Skimmers Corduliidae *Somatochlora*	May-Aug	N: 15-25mm A: 40-60mm	E C W
Whitefaced Skimmers Libellulidae *Leucorrhinia*	Apr-Aug	N: 15-25mm A: 25-40mm	E C W
Skimmers Libellulidae *Libellula*	Apr-Sep	N:20-30mm A: 40-55mm	E C W
Red Skimmers Libellulidae *Sympetrum*	May-Oct	N: 15-30mm A: 30-45mm	E C W

Major Patterns and Tactics for Sprawlers

Stage	Patterns	Ref.	Tactics
Nymph	Assam Dragon	7	8 or 9
	Beaverpelt	2, 8	

(Note: See p. 28 for information on references and p. 32 for information on tactics.)

References

Because of their relatively limited interest to anglers, dragonflies and damselflies have not been treated in a separate angling book. The following texts will be helpful if you wish more technical information.

Cannings, Robert and Kathleen Stuart. *The Dragonflies of British Columbia*. Victoria, B.C.: British Columbia Provincial Museum, 1977.

Corbet, P. S. *A Biology of Dragonflies*. Chicago, Illinois: Quadrangle Books, 1963.

Fabre, J. Henri. *Insect Adventures*. New York: Dodd, Mead and Company, 1917.

Needham, J. G., and M. T. Westfall, Jr. *A Manual of the Dragonflies of North America (Anisoptera)*. Berkeley, California: University of California Press, 1955.

8. Waterbugs: Order Hemiptera

Key to Water Bugs, p. 116

Water bugs belong to the order Hemiptera, also called True Bugs. The majority of Hemiptera are terrestrial insects seen commonly on trees and shrubs. Names like plant bugs, box elder bugs, stink bugs, assassin bugs, and bed bugs describe many common Hemiptera. Terrestrial forms occasionally fall into the water from streamside vegetation and become available to fish. But it is the aquatic Hemiptera, or water bugs, that are of greatest interest and value to fishermen.

Aquatic Hemiptera live either above the water's surface (surface bugs) or below it (underwater bugs). Of the two groups, underwater bugs are more important to the flyfisher because of their availability to fish. This chapter will describe how to recognize these two groups, how they behave, and how best to imitate them.

Note of caution: Some underwater bugs (mainly back swimmers and giant water bugs) can give a painful bite if not handled carefully. Keep them in a net or hold them loosely in your open hand to avoid any problems. The majority of these insects, however, are harmless.

Basic Identification and Similar Orders

One of the distinct characteristics of all Hemiptera is that the nymphs, except for their smaller size and lack of wings, look just like the adults. Nymphs and adults also feed alike and live in the same habitat. Therefore, identification characteristics, except features of the wings, apply to all life stages.

The shape of the mouthparts and wings provide the quickest way to recognize Hemiptera. Mouthparts are needle- or beak-like and are used for piercing and sucking. The length and shape of the mouthparts may vary from quite long and slender to fairly short and rounded. Most are used for piercing plants and sucking sap, but predacious species pierce the skin of their prey and suck out the body fluids.

Wings of Hemiptera are also distinctive. The basal half of the front wings are thick and leathery, while the tips are membranous. When not in use, the front wings lie down over the hind wings and abdomen, providing an effective cover. This type of wing is called a hemelytron (pl. hemelytra). Hemiptera lack tails and have antennae of varying lengths.

The only other insects likely to be confused with water bugs are adult aquatic beetles. The hard, smooth front wings of beetle adults superficially resemble the front wings of Hemiptera. The front wings of Hemiptera, however, are not completely hardened as they are in beetles, and beetles lack needle-like sucking mouthparts.

Size Range

Water bugs come in a wide range of sizes. Small surface forms called broad-shouldered water striders may be only 4-5mm long (3/16"). Long stick-like water scorpions, in contrast, reach lengths of 75mm (3"). Most water bugs range in length from 6-18mm (1/4"-3/4") and are imitated with hook sizes of #16 to #10.

Life Cycle

Hemiptera have incomplete metamorphosis. The similarities between nymphs and adults make changes in the life cycle much less noticeable than they are in other insect orders. There is, for instance, no emergence or drastic change from aquatic nymph to winged adult. Because of this, the timing of nymph to adult development is not important to fishermen, since both nymphs and adults are imitated with the same patterns and tactics. Most water bugs require one year to complete their life cycle.

Stage	Average Duration	Extremes
Egg	1-3 weeks	3-4 months
Nymph	3-8 weeks	3-4 months
Adult	6-8 months	Several weeks to over a year

Unlike most aquatic insects, water bugs spend the largest part of their life cycle as an adult. Eggs are generally laid in the spring on the undersides of aquatic plants or submerged wood debris. Once the eggs hatch, the nymphs develop quickly, changing to adults by early to mid-summer. Adults remain active through the rest of the year, dying after mating and laying eggs the following spring.

Most adult water bugs are good fliers. In the spring, prior to laying eggs, many adults fly in search of new waters to populate. This behavior helps disperse the insects to all available habitats.

North American Distribution and Abundance

Region	# of Families	# of Genera
East	15	42
Central	16	49
West	16	53
Total in N.A.	17	72

Approximate number of North American species: 400 aquatic or semiaquatic species

Habitat Preferences

Water bugs are found in flowing and still waters, but their greatest diversity and abundance occurs in lakes and slow rivers. Most species are associated with aquatic plants, which provide cover and food. They are widely distributed throughout the country. Southern states, where waters remain warm all year, have the largest populations of water bugs.

Identification

The following key applies to both nymphs and adults, since both have similar characteristics. By dividing the order into two simple groups, underwater and surface bugs, pattern selection and tactics can be easily determined.

Key to Water Bugs

This simple key applies to both adults and nymphs, dividing them into two groups, underwater bugs and surface bugs. Differentiation between adults and nymphs is not necessary due to their similarities.

1a. If antennae are longer than head, inserted in front of eyes, and plainly visible from above, it is a SURFACE BUG. Go to p. 117.

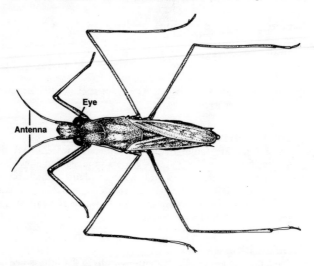

1b. If antennae are shorter than head, inserted beneath the eyes, and not plainly visible from above, it is an UNDERWATER BUG. Go to p. 118.

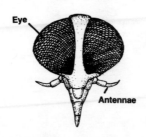

Surface Bugs

Major families and genera of surface bugs:

Families	Genera (# of species)
Gerridae	*Gerris* (15)
(Water Striders)	*Metrobates* (6)
Veliidae	*Microvelia* (18)
(Broad-Shouldered	*Rhagovelia* (9)
Water Striders)	

Surface bugs live totally above water and are therefore often considered semiaquatic, rather than aquatic. "Water striders" (family Gerridae) are the most commonly seen group of surface bugs. The margins of banks and areas around emergent vegetation surrounding lakes and streams provide suitable habitat for most species. One genus of water striders (*Halobates*) lives on the surface of the open ocean along the East and West Coasts.

Surface bugs are predators, feeding on other insects that get trapped in the surface film of the water. Their ability to skate on the water's surface is a continual fascination. Poised on the surface of the water, they would seem an easy meal for fish, but they are rarely eaten. Their defense is apparently a set of stink glands on the side of the body, which spray a repulsive chemical if the insect is attacked.

Major Hatches of Surface Bugs

Surface bugs do not hatch in the normal sense, since nymphs and adults live in the same habitat, have the same behavior, and look similar. Most species are present from early summer through the fall and winter months.

Major Patterns and Tactics for Surface Bugs

Because fish rarely feed on surface bugs, there have been no specific patterns developed to imitate them. Their imitation, if necessary, would provide a difficult problem, however, since the naturals run across the water supported only on the tips of their four hind legs. Thus, a pattern, if it were developed, would be fished by skating it across the surface.

Underwater Bugs

Major families and genera of underwater bugs:

Families	Genera (# of species)
Belostomatidae (Giant Water Bug)	*Belostoma* (8)
Nepidae (Water Scorpions)	*Ranatra* (10)
Naucoridae (Creeping Water Bugs)	*Ambrysus* (13)
	Pelocoris (3)
Corixidae (Water Boatmen)	*Hesperocorixia* (18)
	Trichocorixia (11)
	Sigara (46)
Notonectidae (Back Swimmers)	*Buenoa* (14)
	Notonecta (17)

Underwater bugs are a diverse group of insects. Most are predators. Only the family Corixidae (water boatmen) contain species that are primarily plant feeders. To capture food, some underwater bugs (water scorpions, for example) hang motionless among underwater plants waiting to ambush their prey. The other families swim quickly by kicking their hind legs like oars. These insects actively hunt their food. Once the prey is caught, the underwater bug injects its victim with an enzyme that dissolves protein and turns the tissue into a fluid that is then sucked up through the bug's slender beak.

While these bugs live underwater for most of their lives, they breathe air from the surface. Their air supply is carried underwater as a bubble. When the oxygen in the bubble is depleted they rise to surface for a new one. Depending on the species, water temperature, and activity of the insect, they may remain submerged for one or two minutes or for up to an hour. Some species of the family Naucoridae can remain submerged indefinitely through the use of a **plastron**, a covering of fine hairs on the underside of the thorax and abdomen. Because most species must return periodically to the surface, they live in water no more than three or four feet deep.

Underwater bugs can be very abundant where thick stands of aquatic plants grow along the shores of lakes and rivers. The most common and important groups are the water boatmen and back swimmers. In the late summer and fall, when they are mature and abundant, fish will take them readily. Their active swimming behavior makes it best to imitate them with short twitching retrieves.

Major Hatches of Underwater Bugs

Like the surface bugs, underwater bugs do not hatch. Instead nymphs and adults pass through their life cycle in the same location. The most important time to imitate underwater bugs is in the late summer and fall when they are mature and available to fish. They can also be important food for fish through the winter, since most adults remain active, even under ice.

Major Patterns and Tactics for Underwater Bugs

Stage	Patterns	Ref.	Tactics
Nymph or	Back Swimmer	2, 8	9 or 10
Adult	Water Boatmen	2, 8	

(Note: See p. 28 for information on references and p. 32 for information on tactics.)

References

Hemipterma have not been written about in books exclusively for anglers. The following technical works may be of interest.

Bobb, M. L., *The Aquatic and Semi-Aquatic Hemiptera of Virginia.* Virginia Polytechnic Inst. St. Univ. Res. Div. Bulletin 87, 1974.

Hungerford, H. B., *The Biology and Ecology of Aquatic and Semi-Aquatic Hemiptera.* Kansas: University of Kansas Science Bulletin 21, 1920.

Menke, A. S., ed. *The Semiaquatic and Aquatic Hemiptera of California.* California: Bulletin Calif. Ins. Surv. 21, 1979.

9. Alderflies and Dobsonflies: Order Megaloptera

Key to Megaloptera Larvae, p. 124
Key to Megaloptera Adults, p. 125

The order Megaloptera is one of the least diverse orders of aquatic insects, with only about 40 species in North America. They are found across the country, but their numbers and importance are greatest in the central and eastern states. The order is easily divided into two groups: alderflies and hellgrammites (adults are often called dobsonflies). This chapter will provide information on their identification, habits, and imitation.

Note of caution: Hellgrammites have a large set of mandibles and should be handled gently to avoid being bitten. Keep the insect in a net or hold it loosely in your open hand.

Basic Identification and Similar Orders

Megaloptera larvae are quite distinctive. Most obvious are the long filamentous gills on the sides of the abdomen. The larvae are predators and have well-developed chewing mouthparts. Larvae most closely resemble caddisfly or beetle larvae. Adult Megaloptera are easily confused with other insects, especially adult caddisflies or stoneflies. The following table will help you distinguish these orders.

Identifying Characters	Larvae			
	Alderflies	**Hellgram-mites**	**Caddisflies**	**Beetles**
Anal Hooks	0	4	2	0
Antennae	As long as head	As long as head	Minute	½ to as long as head
Gills	Lateral abdominal filaments	Lateral abdominal filaments	Abdominal filaments present or absent	Abdominal filaments present or absent

Identifying Characters	Alderflies	Adults Hellgram- mites	Caddisflies	Stoneflies
Wings	4, held tent-shaped over abdomen	4, held flat over abdomen	4, held tent-shaped over abdomen	4, held flat over abdomen
Fine Hairs on Wings	None	None	Present	None
Antennae	½-¾ body length	½-¾ body length	1-3 times body length	½ body length
Tails	0	0	0	2, of varying length

Size Range

Megaloptera vary widely in size with hellgrammites growing considerably larger than alderflies. As mature larvae, hellgrammites range from 30-90mm (1 1/4"-3 1/2"), while alderflies range from 12-25mm (1/2"-1"). Adults have a similar size difference. Dobsonflies (hellgrammite adults) range from 40-75mm (1 5/8"-2 3/4"). Alderfly adults are 10-15mm long (3/8"-5/8"). This corresponds to hook sizes of #8 3XL to #4 3XL for hellgrammite patterns and #14 to #8 hooks for alderfly patterns.

Life Cycle

Megaloptera have complete metamorphosis. Most alderflies complete one generation per year. Hellgrammites, on the other hand, normally require two or three years to complete one generation.

Stage	Average Duration	Extremes
Egg	5-10 days	1-3 days to 2-3 weeks
Larva	8 months to 4 years	2 years
Pupa	5-10 days	1 day to 2 weeks
Adult	1-3 days	2-3 months

The majority of the Megaloptera's life cycle is spent in the larval stage. Larvae molt 10 to 11 times during development, which requires eight to nine months for alderflies and two to four years for hellgrammites. Megaloptera larvae are voracious predators throughout their development, feeding on any insects smaller than themselves.

Pupation generally begins in late spring or early summer. Pupae do not develop in the water, however. Instead, the larvae crawl from the water and dig several inches into damp soil near the bank, forming a small chamber or cell in which the pupae develop. Once mature, the pupae dig out of the pupal chambers, and the adults emerge.

Alderfly adults remain close to the bank on trees and shrubs. They can often be seen flying near the water on warm afternoons in the spring and early summer. Dobsonflies, however, are rarely seen even though they are large insects. They are secretive and become active mainly after dark.

Both alderflies and dobsonflies mate on the ground or on foliage. Shortly after mating they begin laying eggs in a most unusual manner. Instead of depositing the eggs in the water, they lay them on objects overhanging the water, such as the undersides of bridges or leaves of trees and shrubs. There the eggs remain for a period of from several days to over a week. When the eggs hatch, the larvae fall into the water to begin their aquatic existence

North American Distribution and Abundance

Region	# of Families	# of Genera
East	2	5
Central	2	4
West	2	6
Total in N.A.	2	8

Approximate number of North American species: 43

Habitat Preferences

Only the larval stage of Megaloptera is aquatic. Both streams and lakes provide suitable habitat, but alderflies and hellgrammites show distinct preferences.

Alderflies prefer lakes or the slow sections of rivers where detritus collects. The larvae are rarely seen, since they spend most of their time crawling through the detritus looking for other insects to eat. Pupae develop out of the water, and adults lay their eggs above water on overhanging objects. Therefore, neither stage is readily available to fish. However, when alderfly adults are abundant along the shoreline foliage, enough of them fall into the water to generate some interest from fish.

Hellgrammites prefer the rocky bottoms of streams and rivers. Some species even live in intermittent streams that may remain dry for several months each year. During dry periods the larvae dig under the streambed where they aestivate until water returns.

Identification

It's only necessary to divide the order Megaloptera into two groups: alderflies (Family: Sialidae) and hellgrammites (Family: Corydalidae). They are easily distinguished from one another as larvae and adults. The following keys provide the specific characteristics for identification.

Key to Megaloptera Larvae

This simple key will help you separate alderfly larvae and dobsonfly larvae (hellgrammites).

1a. If abdominal segments 1-7 have a pair of lateral filaments, and the abdomen ends in a single, long filament; and if length is equal to or less than 25mm (1"), it is an **ALDERFLY**. Go to p. 126.

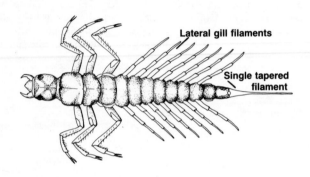

1b. If abdominal segments 1-8 have a pair of lateral filaments, and abdominal segment 10 has a pair of prolegs, each bearing a pair of hooks; and if mature larvae are 30-65mm (1 1/4"-2 1/2") long, it is a **DOBSONFLY** (Hellgrammite). Go to p. 127.

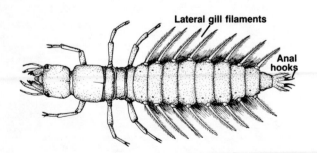

Key to Megaloptera Adults

This simple key will differentiate alderfly and dobsonfly adults.

1a. If insect is less than 25mm (1") long, and head does not have ocelli, it is an ALDERFLY. Go to p. 126.

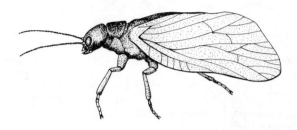

1b. If the insect is larger than 25mm (1") long, and head has ocelli, it is a DOBSONFLY. Go to p. 127.

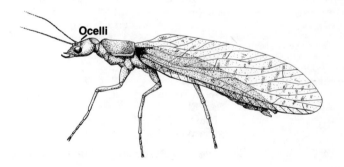

Alderflies

Major families and genera of alderflies:

Families	Genera (# of species)
Sialidae	*Sialis* (23)

Alderflies belong to a single family and genus. The larva's long single gill filament at the tip of the abdomen and its smaller size quickly distinguishes it from a hellgrammite. Adult alderflies are much smaller than dobsonflies, and their wings are dark brown or black and held tent-shaped over the abdomen.

The adult stage is the more important stage to imitate. Larvae remain well hidden in bottom detritus and provide little opportunity for fish to feed on them. Adults, however, are poor fliers and are often concentrated on the foliage near the water. It only takes a slight breeze to blow enough adults into the water to entice fish. A dry fly or wet fly fished dead drift or with a slow hand-twist retrieve near shoreline vegetation will normally produce well on such occasions.

Major Hatches of Alderflies

Name	Emergence	Size	Dist.
Alderfly	Apr-Jul	L:10-25mm	E C W
Sialis sp.		P:10-15mm	
		A:10-15mm	

Major Patterns and Tactics for Alderflies

Stage	Patterns	Ref.	Tactics
Larva	Woolly Worm	8	2, 9
Adult	Dark Elk		
	Hair Caddis	8	6 or 8
	Alder Wet Fly	8	2 or 9

(Note: See p. 28 for information on references and p. 32 for information on tactics.)

Dobsonflies

Major families and genera of dobsonflies:

Families	**Genera (# of species)**
Corydalidae	*Corydalus* (2)
	Chauliodes (2)
	Dysmicohermes (2)
	Neohermes (5)
	Protochauliodes (6)

One family and five major genera make up this group of aquatic insects. As a whole, they are distributed across the country, but they're much more common and important in fishing east of the Rocky Mountains, where the larvae are frequently used as bait by smallmouth bass fishermen. Larvae are easily recognized by their large size and by the four anal hooks at the tip of their abdomen.

Hellgrammites are some of the fiercest predators of the underwater world. Not only are most other aquatic insects fair game, but small fish and tadpoles are also readily eaten. The larvae actively roam the rocky bottoms of streams and rivers and are often available to fish. The larva's long life span further increases their availability. Numerous nymph patterns have been developed to imitate the larvae as they crawl along the bottom. Fish them dead drift right on the bottom of rocky riffles or runs.

Adult hellgrammites or dobsonflies are rarely seen due to their short existence (only 1-3 days) and their nocturnal habits. Their appearance can be striking, however. The wings are quite large with a mottled brown and gray pattern, and some males possess tusks half as long as their body. These tusks are apparently important during courtship or mating. The secretive habits of adults, however, make them a rare food for fish and unimportant to imitate.

Major Hatches of Hellgrammites

Name	**Emergence**	**Size**	**Dist.**
Hellgrammite	Apr-Aug	L:30-90mm	E C W
or Dobsonfly		P:30-75mm	
Corydalidae		A:30-75mm	

Major Patterns and Tactics for Hellgrammites

Stage	Patterns	Ref.	Tactics
Larva	Woolly Worm	2, 8	1 or 2
	Hellgrammite		
	Nymph		

(Note: See p. 28 for information on references and p. 32 for information on tactics.)

References

There are no books that deal exclusively with this order. Books that contain chapters about this group are listed here.

Chandler, H.P. *The Aquatic Insects of California.* Berkeley, California: University of California Press, 1956.

McCafferty, W. Patrick. *Aquatic Entomology.* Boston: Science Books International, 1981.

10. Caddisflies: Order Trichoptera

Caddisflies present a difficult challenge to flyfishers and aquatic biologists alike. This challenge is a direct result of their abundance and diversity. The abundance of caddisflies can be staggering. Hatches sometimes blanket the sky and produce frenzied feeding by fish. For the flyfisher, caddis activity can result in exceptional fishing if the correct patterns and tactics are used. The diversity of caddisflies make them important in nearly every freshwater habitat throughout North America. There are more caddisfly species than all species of mayflies and stoneflies combined— over 1,200 species in North America.

There is no simple way to categorize and describe the caddisflies. Their abundance makes them constantly important to flyfishermen, but their diversity makes it difficult to identify and recognize specific groups. To provide the angler with a simplified, yet useful, approach to caddisflies, this chapter breaks the order into five groups based on larval behavior. The information provided in this chapter will help you know where and when caddis occur and how to imitate them.

Basic Identification and Similar Orders

Caddis larvae are best known for the unique cases most species build. The moth-like adults have no striking features, but all species have wings covered with fine silky hairs from which the order's name Trichoptera (Tricos = hair, Optera = wing) is derived. The keys in Chapter 4 give the identifying characteristics of caddis larvae and adults. While the pupae are not described in a key in this chapter, they can be recognized by their long legs and antennae, wing pads that slope down and under their thorax and abdomen, and the absence of tails.

Insects most often mistaken for caddis larvae include alderflies, hellgrammites, and some beetle and Diptera larvae. Adult caddisflies are frequently confused with adult alderflies, stoneflies, or moths. The following table will help you distinguish these insects.

Larvae

Identifying Characters	Caddis	Alderflies	Hellgram-mites	Beetles	Diptera
Thoracic Legs(pairs)	3	3	3	3	0
Anal Hooks	2	0	4	0	0
Antennae	Minute	As long as head	As long as head	½ to as long as head	Minute
Gills	Abdominal filaments may be present or absent	Lateral abdominal filaments	Lateral abdominal filaments	Filaments of variable size and placement	Filaments of variable size and placement

Adults

Identifying Characters	Caddis	Alderflies	Stoneflies	Moths
Wings	4, held tent-shaped with fine hairs	4, held tent-shaped, no fine hairs	4, held flat over abdomen	4, held flat over abdomen, with scale-like hairs
Antennae	1-3 times body length	½-¾ body length	½ body length	½-¾ body length
Ocelli	3 or none	none	3 or 2	2
Tails	0	0	2	0

Size Range

With such diversity it's not surprising that caddisflies exhibit a wide range of sizes. The larvae show the largest size range. The tiny microcaddis (Family: Hydroptilidae) are only 3-4mm long (1/8"), while the largest case builders have cases up to 60mm (2 1/2") long. Adults may range from 2-3mm (1/16") up to 35mm (1 3/8") from the head to the tip of the wings. Such a wide range of sizes might require patterns tied on hooks from a #26 to a #4 4XL. The most common and important hook sizes for caddis range from #16 to #8.

Life Cycle

Caddisflies go through complete metamorphosis, which means they pass through four stages of development: egg, larva, pupa, and adult. Most species pass through one complete generation per year. The length of time spent in each stage, however, varies considerably with different species and geographic areas. A few species complete two generations a year, while others require two years to complete one generation.

Stage	Average Duration	Extremes
Egg	2-4 weeks	8-9 months
Larva	6-10 months	1-2 months to 18 months
Pupa	2-5 weeks	2-3 months
Adult	1-4 weeks	3-4 months

As with most aquatic insects, the majority of the life cycle is spent in the larval stage. During their development, caddis larvae pass through only five instars. (A couple of species have been found with six.) As they grow, case builders must make their cases larger as well. This may be done by building a new case after each molt or by adding on to the existing case. Most species simply add on to the existing case. Water temperature and food supply are the major factors affecting how long the larval stage lasts.

Cased caddis may seem well-protected inside their cases of twigs or gravel, but fish frequently eat them, case and all. There are also many species of caddis larvae that build no case. These species are readily eaten by fish, and their imitations make excellent patterns.

The pupal stage develops inside the larval case. Larvae that build no cases construct a rough shelter prior to pupation. The pupae are well-protected inside the case and are not available to feeding fish until they begin emerging. To emerge, the mature pupae first cut out of their protective shelter and, if in a stream, begin drifting along the bottom. Depending on the species, the pupae may drift from four to over 20 feet, providing fish an easy meal. Finally they begin their ascent to the surface by using their hind legs as swimming paddles and by expelling gas bubbles under the pupal exoskeleton.

The emerging pupa is technically called a pharate adult. This term is used because the insect is not really a pupa anymore, but rather an adult that is covered by the sack-like skin of the pupa. Once at the surface, the pupal skin splits open, and the completely developed adult flies quickly away. The emerging pupa (or pharate adult) is one of the most vulnerable stages during the caddis life cycle and is one of the best stages for flyfishers to imitate.

The adult stage provides the next opportunity for fish to eat caddis. Most adults fly so quickly off the surface after emergence that fish concentrate their feeding during a hatch on the rising pupae. However, some adults, commonly called Travelling Sedges, run across the water's surface for hundreds of feet to reach shore instead of flying. This behavior creates an exciting opportunity for dry-fly fishing.

Once on shore, the adults mate on streamside foliage. After mating, the females return to the water to lay their eggs and are again available to feeding fish. Some species oviposit on the water's surface by releasing clusters of eggs as their abdomen touches the water. Others dive into the water and swim to the bottom where the eggs are attached. After laying all their eggs, they struggle back to the surface. Fish readily take the females on the surface or underwater. Many flyfishers use only dry flies, even though imitating the submerged females with soft hackles or wet flies could increase their success dramatically.

North American Distribution and Abundance

Region	# of Families	# of Genera
East	18	83
Central	14	59
West	21	108
Total in N.A.	22	143

Approximate number of North American species: 1,200

Habitat Preferences

Caddisflies are common in nearly all freshwater habitats. Home may be a high, cold mountain stream or a small temporary pond. Their abundance in both flowing and still waters makes them important to flyfishermen in all areas of North America.

Even though they have adapted to most aquatic habitats, the earliest, most primitive caddisflies are thought to have evolved in cool flowing waters, with new species gradually adapting to warm still waters. This theory is partially born out by the fact that of the 22 North American families of caddis, all 22 have some representatives in cool streams, 20 are represented in warm rivers, seven occur in lakes or ponds, and only three are represented in temporary pools. There are hundreds of species in warm rivers and lakes, however, which shows how well caddisflies have adapted to these habitats.

Identification

Caddisflies present a difficult identification problem, whether you're a professional trying to identify them to genus or species or a flyfisher trying to determine their basic group or family. To make their identification as simple and useful as possible, the following keys separate caddis larvae and adults into one of five groups based on larval behavior: free-living caddis, net-spinning caddis, saddle-case caddis, purse-case caddis, and tube-case caddis. Although patterns and tactics specified for one of these groups will often work equally well for others, dividing them into these groups allows some important distinctions to be made that could not be made otherwise.

Adult caddis present the greatest problems. Even identifying them to one of the five groups can be difficult. For accuracy, the key uses characteristics of the mouthparts (specifically the maxillary palpi) which are small and difficult to see. A magnifying lens will generally be needed to see them clearly. Because adult caddis all have the same basic shape, the same fly patterns can be varied in size and color to cover most hatches. However, identification to one of the five groups will help determine specific behaviors that can be important in selecting the best tactic and presentation.

No key to the pupa is presented because of the difficulties in their collection and identification. Determining which group a pupa belongs to can best be done by association with the adults collected during a hatch. Because pupa are so important for flyfishers to imitate and because their color can be difficult to determine, a pupa color summary chart for the major families and genera follows the keys.

Key to Caddisfly Larvae

Deciding which type of caddisfly you have collected depends in part on whether the insect is found living freely or living in some kind of case. In addition, some species live in a "fixed retreat" and build a capture net. This net is often destroyed during collection, so careful observation is vital.

1a. If larva is found without a portable case, and either lives in a fixed retreat* or is completely free-living, go to **2**.

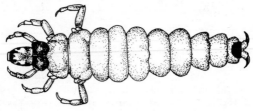

1b. If larva is in a portable case* of mineral or plant material, go to **3**.

2a. If larva is in a fixed retreat with a capture net present (note: net often destroyed when larva is collected), and head is as wide as thorax; and if last abdominal segment does not have a dorsal plate, and the insect is found in running water (almost exclusively), it is a NET-SPINNING CADDIS. Go to p. 143.

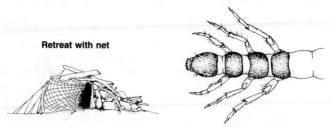

Retreat with net

2b. If larva is without any type of retreat or net, and head is often narrower than thorax; and if last abdominal segment has a dorsal plate, and specimen is found in running water, it is a FREE-LIVING CADDIS. Go to p. 141.

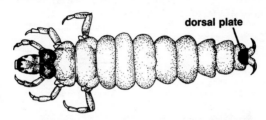

3a. If larval case is typically tubular or rectangular in shape, and head and legs of larva protrude from front of case when crawling; and if size of mature larva is 9-37mm (3/8"-1 1/2"), it is a TUBE-CASE CADDIS. Go to p. 149.

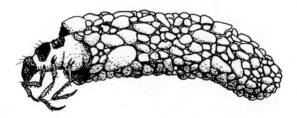

3b. If larval case is shaped differently, and body size is generally smaller, go to 4.

*During pupation, caddisfly cases will be attached to the substrate and may appear as fixed retreats.

4a. If larval case is dome- or igloo-shaped and made of fine gravel, and larva is not visible when viewed from above but both ends of larva protrude from case when viewed from bottom; and if body length is small, 4-9mm (1/8"-3/8"), and larva was found in a stream or river (almost exclusively), it is a SADDLE-CASE CADDIS. Go to p. 146.

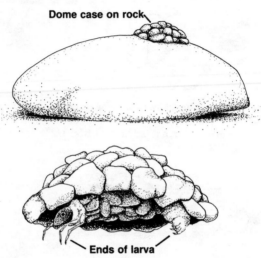

Dome case on rock

Ends of larva

4b. If mature larvae are very small, 2-5mm (1/16"-3/16"), and final instar larvae are found in typically flat, purse-shaped cases made of fine silk and sand grains; and if abdomen is often greatly expanded and without gills, and all thoracic segments have well-developed dorsal plates, it is a PURSE-CASE OR MICROCADDIS. Go to p. 148.

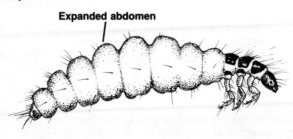

Expanded abdomen

Key to Caddisfly Adults

Identification of caddisfly adults to families is among the most difficult tasks for the amateur entomologist. For the most part, knowing the type of adult caddis is not important to fishing success, since adult caddisfly patterns imitate all types of caddis equally well. Color and size are the most important determinations to make. However, if you wish to identify the insect by the groups below, careful observation and measurements are necessary.

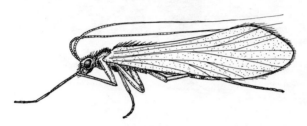

1a. If the insect is very small, usually less than 5mm (3/16") from head to tip of wing, and the hind wing is narrow, pointed, and has a posterior fringe of long, fine hairs, it is a PURSE-CASE OR MICROCADDIS. Go to p. 148.

Hind wing

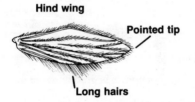

Pointed tip

Long hairs

1b. If the insect is larger, typically longer than 5mm (3/16"), go to **2**.

METRIC 1 2 3 4 5 6 7 8 9

2a. If maxillary palpi are 5-segmented, and the fifth segment is flexible and at least twice as long as the fourth, it is a NET-SPIN-NING CADDIS. Go to p. 143.

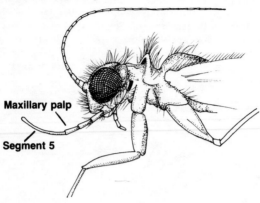

Maxillary palp

Segment 5

2b. If maxillary palpi are 3-, 4-, or 5-segmented, and if 5-segmented, fifth segment is similar in shape and length to the fourth, go to **3**.

Maxillary palp

Segment 5

3a. If top of head (dorsum) has 3 ocelli, go to **4**.

3b. If dorsum lacks ocelli, it is a TUBE-CASE CADDIS. Go to p. 149.

4a. If maxillary palpi are 5-segmented with second segment short, round, and approximately the same length as the first, go to **5**.

Maxillary palp

Segment 2

4b. If maxillary palpi are 3-, 4-, or 5-segmented, and if 5-segmented, second segment is slender and longer than first, it is a TUBE-CASE CADDIS. Go to p. 149.

Maxillary palp

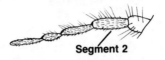

Segment 2

5a. If tibia of front legs has preapical spur, it is a FREE-LIVING CADDIS. Go to p. 141.

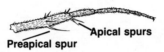

Apical spurs

Preapical spur

5b. If tibia of front legs has no preapical spur, it is a SADDLE-CASE CADDIS. Go to p. 146.

Tibia

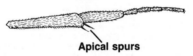

Apical spurs

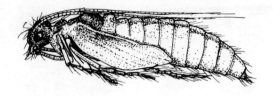

Caddisfly Pupa Color Summary Chart

Caddis Group	Yellow	Brown	Orange	Green	Gray	Black
Free-Living Caddis						
Rhyacophilidae						
Rhyacophila		X		X		
Net-Spinning Caddis						
Philopotamidae						
Chimarra						X
Dolophilodes		X				
Wormalidia		X		X		
Psychomyiidae						
Psychomyia		X				
Polycentropodidae						
Nyctiophylax	X	X				
Polycentropus	X	X				
Hydropsychidae						
Arctopsyche				X	X	
Cheumatopsyche		X		X		
Hydrospyche	X	X				
Macrostemum		X				
Saddle-Case Caddis						
Glossosamtidae						
Glossosoma		X		X		
Purse-Case Caddis						
Hydroptilidae						
Hydroptila	X	X	X			
Oxyethira	X	X				
Tube-Case Caddis						
Brachycentridae						
Amiocentrus				X		
Brachycentrus				X		

	Yellow	Brown	Orange	Green	Gray	Black
Lepidostomatidae						
Lepidostoma		X				
Leptoceridae						
Mystacides						X
Oecetis		X				
Ceraclea		X				
Limnephilidae						
Pycnopsyche		X			X	
Chryanda	X	X				
Hydatophylax		X			X	
Limnephilus		X			X	
Dicosmoecus		X				
Neophylax	X	X				
Odonoceridae						
Psilotreta				X	X	
Molannidae						
Molanna		X			X	
Phryganeidae						
Banksiola	X	X			X	
Ptilostomis	X	X				

Free-Living Caddis

Major families and genera of free-living caddis:
Families   **Genera (# of species)**
Rhyacophilidae   *Rhyacophila* (100+)

Free-living caddis are considered one of the most primitive types of caddis because the larvae build no case. Instead they are completely exposed to the elements and make a juicy meal for hungry trout. Besides the lack of a case, larvae can be recognized by their large anal hooks. Many species are a bright green color and are commonly called Green Rock Worms. Not all are green, however; some are shades of brown or gray. Gills may be present as finger-like filaments on the abdomen or may be completely absent. The larvae range in size from 7-17mm (1/4"-3/4").

The pupae develop inside a gravel shelter constructed by the larvae prior to pupation. Three to five weeks are generally required for the pupae to mature. Pupae tend to be green to brown in color, and range in size from 9-17mm (3/8"-3/4").

Adults are approximately the same size as the pupae. Body colors range from greenish-gray or brown with brownish or gray wings. To confirm the identification of adults, look to see that they have five segmented maxillary palpi and three ocelli.

Free-living caddis live exclusively in streams and rivers. Cool mountain streams generally harbor the best populations. As streams grow larger and warmer, the numbers of free-living caddis decline. Their need for cool, well-oxygenated water also forces them to live in the rocky riffle areas of streams. The larvae are predacious, and while they crawl over the bottom in search of food, they are commonly washed into the current where they become readily available to fish. Larval patterns should be fished carefully through riffles with upstream casts and a strike indicator; fish take the larvae with a very subtle strike.

Pupation occurs in the same riffle habitat that the larvae live in. Thus, even though the pupae are excellent swimmers, they drift downstream in the swift currents as they swim to the surface to emerge, again providing easy meals for fish. Unlike some caddis which emerge at night, free-living caddis most often emerge in the afternoon. Pupal patterns are the best type to use during a hatch. Cast them down and across so they rise up to the surface like a natural pupa.

Adult behavior makes them readily available to fish, too. During emergence most fish will take rising pupae. But when the females return to lay their eggs, they swim or crawl to the bottom and attach strings of eggs on the sides of rocks. After laying all their eggs, they drift slowly back to the surface. Fish will feed on them as they swim to the bottom or on their slow return to the surface. Most flyfishermen use adult patterns dry on the surface and, therefore, overlook the adult's importance underwater while they lay their eggs. Fishing submerged wet flies or soft hackle flies when adults lay their eggs can provide exciting fishing.

Major Hatches of Free-Living Caddis

Name	Emergence	Size	Dist.
Green Sedge or	May-Jul	L: 11-20mm	E C W
Green Rock Worm	and	P: 8-16mm	
Rhyacophila	Aug-Oct	A: 8-16mm	

Major Patterns and Tactics for Free-Living Caddis

Stage	Patterns	Ref.	Tactics
Larva	Green Rock Worm	2, 8, 11	1
	Latex Caddis	2	
	Zug Bug	2, 8	
Pupa	Soft Hackle	10	2, 3, 5
	Flymph	4	
	Sparkle Pupa	2	
	Tied-Down Caddis	2	
Adult Dry	Elk Hair Caddis	2, 8	6 or 7
	Kings River Caddis	2, 8	
	Woodchuck Caddis	2, 8	
	Henryville Special	8	
Adult Wet	Dark Cahill Wet	2	2, 3 or 5
	March Brown Wet	2	
	Flymph	4	

(Note: See p. 28 for information on references and p. 32 for information on tactics.)

Net-Spinning Caddis

Major families and genera of net-spinning caddis:

Families	Genera (# of species)
Philopotamidae	*Chimarra* (17)
	Dolophilodes (8)
	Wormaldia (13)
Psychomyiidae	*Psychomyia* (3)
Polycentropodidae	*Nyctiophylax* (8)
	Polycentropus (40)
Hydropsychidae	*Arctopsyche* (4)
	Parapsyche (7)
	Cheumatopsyche (40)
	Hydropsyche (43)
	Macrostemum (3)

The net-spinning caddis are an abundant and diverse group with more than 200 species found in streams and rivers throughout the country. All the families and genera listed above can at times be important, but the family Hydropsychidae is consistently the most important for flyfishers to imitate.

The larvae are not true case builders. Instead, most build a crude retreat or shelter of twigs, leaves, or gravel which is firmly attached to the sides of rocks. All spin some type of net, similar to a spider web, used to filter food out of the water. The nets are generally attached to the front of the larval shelter but are seldom seen since they collapse when the shelters are lifted from the stream.

Net-spinning larvae, pupae, and adults are similar in appearance to free-living caddis. The larvae have the same form and color, but can be separated by the characteristics given in the Key to Caddisfly Larvae. Mature net-spinning larvae range in size from 5-25mm (3/16"-1"). Most are between 12-18mm (1/2"-3/4"). Pupae develop in the larval retreats. They may be shades of green, brown, yellow, or gray, and like the free-living pupae, they swim actively to the surface during emergence. Adults closely resemble the free-living caddisfly adults in size and color. The maxillary palpi of adult net-spinning caddis have a unique shape, and all but one family (Philopotamidae) lack ocelli.

In many streams the net-spinners are the most abundant and important caddisfly present. They can be equally abundant in the riffle areas of cool rapid streams and in moderately flowing areas of large rivers. In fact, the size and structure of the capture nets of the different species are adapted to specific sizes of streams. Some species also occur along the wave-washed shorelines of lakes. In many instances dams have created an artificial but ideal situation for net-spinning caddis. Zooplankton and phytoplankton often reach large populations in the reservoirs behind dams. When this rich food supply goes over the dam into the river, it provides a perfect food source for these caddis.

All stages of the net-spinning caddis are important to imitate. While the larvae may appear somewhat protected from fish in their larval shelters, they are often abundant in stream drift and make excellent models for imitation. Larval patterns are best fished through moderate to fast riffle areas. Sunrise and sunset can be periods of heavy drift by the larvae, and therefore, good times for nymphing.

The pupae develop in the larval shelters. After three to five weeks in the case, the pupae break free and swim to the surface where the adults emerge. The pupae's exposure in open water makes them easy targets for fish. The fish often feed selectively on pupae at these times, so choosing a pupal pattern is often critical for success.

Adults reach their greatest importance to flyfishermen during egg laying. Like the free-living caddis adults, the females dive into the water and swim to the bottom where they deposit their eggs under rocks. When all eggs are laid, they let go of the bottom and struggle back to the surface. Egg laying activity typically occurs in the afternoon or evening and presents the perfect opportunity to use wet flies or submerged dry patterns when surface patterns fail to produce.

Major Hatches of Net-Spinning Caddis

Name	Emergence	Size	Dist.
Little Black Sedge Philopotamidae *Chimarra*	Apr-Jun	L: 7-10mm P: 6-8mm A: 6-8mm	E C
Little Autumn Stream Sedge Philopotamidae *Wormaldia*	Apr-Jun and Aug-Oct	L: 8-12mm P: 8-10mm A: 8-10mm	E C W
Dinky Purple- Breasted Sedge Psychomyiidae *Psychomyia*	Jun-Aug	L: 5-8mm P: 4-6mm A: 4-6mm	E C W
Brown Checkered Summer Sedge Polycentropodidae *Polycentropus*	Jun-Aug	L: 8-12mm P: 9-11mm A: 9-11mm	E C W
Great Gray Spotted Sedge Hydropsychidae *Arctopsyche*	Jun-Jul	L: 18-25mm P: 15-20mm A: 15-20mm	E W
Little Spotted Sedge Hydropsychidae *Cheumatopsyche*	Apr-Jul	L: 8-12mm P: 8-10mm A: 8-10mm	E C W
Spotted Sedge Hydropsychidae *Hydropsyche*	May-Jun	L: 10-15mm P: 10-14mm A: 10-14mm	E C W

METRIC 1 2 3 4 5 6 7 8 9

Major Patterns and Tactics for Net-Spinning Caddis

Stage	Patterns	Ref.	Tactics
Larva	Zug Bug	2, 8	1
	Latex Caddis	2	
	Herl Nymph	2	
Pupa	Soft Hackle	10	2, 3, or 5
	Flymph	4	
	Sparkle Pupa	2	
Adult Dry	Elk Hair Caddis	2, 8	6 or 7
	Kings River Caddis	2, 8	
	Woodchuck Caddis	2, 8	
	Henryville Special	8	
Adult Wet	Flymph	4	2, 3 or 5
	Gray Sedge Wet	8	
	Dark Cahill Wet	2	

(Note: See p. 28 for information on references and p. 32 for information on tactics.)

Saddle-Case Caddis

Major families and genera of saddle-case caddis:

Families	Genera (# of species)
Glossosomatidae	*Agapetus* (30)
	Glossosoma (25)

The saddle-case caddis belong to a single family that contains nearly 80 species. Like the free-living caddis, they are a primitive group. The larvae build a unique dome-shaped case. This is different than the tubular cases of the true case builders, but it does provide protection for the larva and appears to be the first step in the evolution of more refined case building.

The distinctive case is probably the easiest way to identify larvae of this group. The name "saddle-case" refers to the design of the case— it completely covers the larva from above, but when viewed from below both ends of the larva protrude from the case and a narrow strap or "saddle" crosses under the larva. The larvae lack gills, are tan to yellowish-pink in color, and are only 5-8mm (3/16"-3/8") in length.

Pupation occurs under the dome-like case. Pupae are small and range from brown to green in color. Adults are also small and except for their smaller size, are almost identical to free-living caddis adults. The only other difference between these two groups is that saddle-case adults lack a preapical spur on their forelegs, which is present on free-living caddis adults.

Saddle-case caddis are inhabitants of flowing waters. The riffle areas of small to large streams provide plenty of room for the larvae to crawl over the bottom rocks where they scrape off periphyton, the thin slippery layer of diatoms. Their feeding strips off the algae, leaving a trail of bare rock behind them. Larvae often congregate along the margins of riffles forming dense colonies prior to pupation and resulting in concentrated hatches when the pupae emerge.

The larvae are more important to imitate than they may seem. Their cases offer good protection and are held tightly to the rocks, but as the larvae grow, they leave their cases periodically to build bigger ones. Large numbers of larvae may drift in the current at these times, providing a perfect opportunity to fish a small larval pattern. May through July can be a period of rapid growth and high drift for the larvae.

Pupae and adults are also important to imitate. Pupae swim actively in the current to reach the surface, and their concentrated hatches often cause selective feeding. The adults, although small, swim to the stream bottom to lay their eggs. This makes them very available to fish and important to imitate with wet fly patterns.

Major Hatches of Saddle-Case Caddis

Name	Emergence	Size	Dist.
Little Tan	Apr-Jun	L: 5-8mm	E C W
Short-Horn Sedge	and	P: 5-8mm	
Glossosomatidae	Jul-Oct	A: 6-10mm	
Glossosoma			

Major Patterns and Tactics for Saddle-Case Caddis

Stage	Patterns	Ref.	Tactics
Larva	Latex Caddis	2	1
Pupa	Soft Hackle	10	3 or 5
	Flymph	4	
	Little Green Caddis	2	
Adult Dry	Elk Hair Caddis	2, 8	6 or 7
	Henryville Special	8	
Adult Wet	Flymph	4	2, 3, or 5
	Light Cahill Wet	2	

(Note: See p. 28 for information on references and p. 32 for information on tactics.)

Purse-Case Caddis

Major families and genera of purse-case caddis:

Families	Genera (# of species)
Hydroptilidae	*Hydroptila* (60)
	Oxyethira (30)
	Ochrotrichia (42)

While there is only a single family in this group, it is very diverse, with almost 200 known species. Besides being known as purse-case caddis, these insects are also commonly called microcaddis because of their minute size (2-5mm, 1/16"-3/16"). These caddis are so small that size alone is a major identifying characteristic.

Larvae are free-living until they reach their fifth and final instar. They then build a purse-shaped case of silk and fine grains of sand. The actual shapes of the cases vary from thin, slipper-like cases to slender, bottle-shaped cases. Most larvae also have an extremely enlarged abdomen, which gives them a distinctive appearance.

Pupae and adults are best recognized by their minute size. Pupae vary in color from yellow to brown to orange. Adults have slender pointed hind wings with a fringe of long hairs (see Key to Caddisfly Adults). Colors range from yellow or brown to green with brown or tan mottled wings.

Purse-case caddis are found in nearly all types of water and are very tolerant of warm water. Moderate to slow currents in rivers often have dense populations. Larvae prefer bottoms with fine sand or aquatic plants. In streams with thermal springs, like the Firehole River, they can be one of the most abundant insects.

The tiny size of these caddis means they are often overlooked by flyfishers. During emergence and egg laying, however, they can be extremely important to imitate. The pupae commonly drift long distances in the surface film, and the fish taking them create smutting rises, which are often mistaken for the riseforms of fish taking midges. Adults dive underwater to lay their eggs. This generally occurs in slack water, where they become easy, concentrated meals for fish.

Major Hatches of Purse-Case Caddis

Name	Emergence	Size	Dist.
Vari-Colored	Jun-Aug	L: 3-5mm	E C W
Microcaddis		P: 3-4mm	
Hydroptila		A: 3-4mm	
Cream and Brown	Jun-Sep	L: 2-4mm	E C W
Microcaddis		P: 2-3mm	
Oxyethira		A: 2-5mm	

Major Patterns and Tactics for Purse-Case Caddis

Stage	Patterns	Ref.	Tactics
Larva	Generally not important to imitate.		
Pupa	Soft Hackle	10	2 or 4
	Flymph	4	
	Emergent Sparkle Pupa	2	
Adult Dry	Elk Hair Caddis	2, 8	6 or 7
	Fluttering Caddis	2	
Adult Wet	Flymph	4	4 or 5

(Note: See p. 28 for information on references and p. 32 for information on tactics.)

Tube-Case Caddis

Major families and genera of tube-case caddis:

Families	Genera (# of species)
Brachycentridae	*Amiocentrus* (1)
	Brachycentrus (9)
Lepidostomatidae	*Lepidostoma* (65)
Leptoceridae	*Mystacides* (3)
	Oecetis (34)
Limnephilidae	*Pycnopsyche* (16)
	Chyranda (1)
	Hydatophylax (4)
	Frenesia (2)
	Platycentropus (3)
	Limnephilus (100 +)
	Hesperophylax (6)
	Psychoglpha (15)
	Dicosmoecus (4)
	Onocosmoecus (6)
	Oligophlebodes (7)
	Neophylax (15)

Families	**Genera (# of species)**
Odontoceridae	*Psilotreta* (7)
Molannidae	*Molanna* (5)
Phryganeidae	*Banksiola* (5)
	Pyryganea (2)
	Ptilostomis (4)

From the list above it's easy to see what a complex group this is. There is a tremendous array of families, genera, and species occuring in a great variety of sizes and colors. The larvae of all these species, though, build a tube-like case around their abdomen which they carry with them wherever they go. Cased-caddis larvae go by many local names; periwinkle or masonry worms are two examples.

The portable cases make the larvae of this group easy to recognize. Cases vary widely in shape and in the material used. Some are finely constructed of sand grains or gravel, while others look like broken bits of leaves or twigs. Many genera can be recognized simply by the type of case they build, but in general, identification of larvae beyond family becomes quite difficult. Cased larvae vary widely in size, ranging from 7-60mm (1/4"-over 2"). Colors of larvae (not the case) are typically yellow, brown, or shades of green on the abdomen and brown or black on the head and thorax.

As the larvae grow, they tend to enlarge their cases rather than abandon them. At times they may abandon their cases to escape predators or because of damage. A new case will then be constructed within a few hours. The larvae will generally not survive for more than a day or two if unable to build a new case.

Most larvae reach maturity in six to eight months, at which time they attach their case to the substrate, seal both ends and transform to a pupa. The pupae are well protected inside the larval case and require from two weeks to over three months to fully mature.

Identification of pupae even to family can be quite difficult. It can be simplified, in part, by noting the type of case the pupa is developing in, but this distinction still requires considerable experience. The flyfisher's main concern is the insect's size and color. The pupal color summary chart shows that the major colors are shades of yellow, brown, green, and gray. Determining a pupa's color is best done by opening a case and removing the pupa. If it's a mature pupa its wing pads will be dark brown or black. Sizes may range from 6-34mm (1/4"-1 1/2") in length.

Adult tube-case caddis also vary widely in size and color. All species, however, lack ocelli, the small round eye spots in the middle of the head. Identifying adult tube-case caddis to family or genus is almost an impossibility without a microscope, technical keys, and some luck.

The evolution of a case has allowed these caddis to survive in nearly all freshwater habitats. Some make their home in the fast riffles of mountain streams; others live in slower, warmer rivers with bottoms of sand or plant debris. In lakes and ponds, tube-case caddis are the only caddis that become abundant enough to consistently interest fish and fishermen.

All stages of tube-case caddis are taken by fish. Fishermen often overlook the importance of the larvae, but fish don't. They will take larvae, cases and all. Some cased caddis drift in rivers in very high numbers (family Brachycentridae, for example). This makes them readily available to fish and, therefore, useful models for imitation.

Pupae become very important to imitate when they leave the larval case and swim to the surface to emerge. Many cased caddis pupae emerge at night. Early morning, however, is an excellent time to fish a pattern imitating a night-emerging pupa, since some may still be emerging, and fish often continue to look for them.

Like other caddis, adults are useful to imitate during a hatch or when they return to the water to lay their eggs on the water's surface. Imitating them with dry flies fished dead drift or with a skating action can result in excellent catches. No matter where you live or what kind of water you fish, some cased caddis will be important to imitate.

Major Hatches of Tube-Case Caddis

Name	Emergence	Size	Dist.
American Grannom	Apr-May	L: 12-17mm	E C W
Brachycentridae	and	P: 10-13mm	
Brachycentrus	Jul-Aug	A: 10-13mm	
Little Plain	Jun-Sep	L: 10-15mm	E C W
Brown Sedge		P: 8-10mm	
Lepidostomatidae		A: 8-10mm	
Lepidostoma			

Name	Emergence	Size	Dist.
Long Horn Sedge Leptoceridae *Oecetis*	May-Sep	L: 10-15mm P: 9-12mm A: 9-12mm	E C W
Great Brown Autumn Sedge Limnephilidae *Pycnopsyche*	Aug-Oct	L: 40-60mm P: 18-25mm A: 18-25mm	E C
Pale Western Stream Sedge Limnephilidae *Chyranda*	Aug-Oct	L: 20-35mm P: 12-18mm A: 18-25mm	W
Giant Cream Sedge Limnephilidae *Hydatophylax*	Aug-Oct	L: 50-75mm P: 25-34mm A: 25-34mm	E C W
Summer Flier Sedge Limnephilidae *Limnephilus*	Jul-Sep	L: 30-50mm P: 13-20mm A: 13-20mm	E C W
Giant Orange Sedge Limnephilidae *Dicosmoecus*	Sep-Nov	L: 25-40mm P: 20-25mm A: 20-30mm	W
Little Western Dark Sedge Limnephilidae *Oligophlebodes*	Aug-Sep	L: 7-9mm P: 5-7mm A: 6-8mm	W
Autumn Mottled Sedge Limnephilidae *Neophylax*	Sep-Nov	L: 10-20mm P: 10-14mm A: 10-15mm	E C W
Gray Checkered Sedge Molannidae *Molanna*	May-Aug	L: 15-27mm P: 10-16mm A: 10-16mm	E C W
Dark Blue Sedge Odontoceridae *Psilotreta*	Apr-Jun	L: 15-20mm P: 10-13mm A: 12-15mm	E
Travelling Sedge Phryganeidae *Banksiola*	Jun-Jul	L: 35-45mm P: 15-20mm A: 18-25mm	E C W

Name	Emergence	Size	Dist.
Rush Sedge	Jun-Aug	L: 35-45mm	E C W
Phryganeidae		P: 15-20mm	
Phryganea		A: 20-30mm	

Major Patterns and Tactics for Tube-Case Caddis

Stage	Patterns	Ref.	Tactics
Larva	Strawman	2	1 or 8
	Tan Caddis Larva	8	
	Little Gray Caddis	8	
Pupa	Soft Hackle	10	5, 9, or 10
	Flymph	4	
	Sparkle Pupa	2	
	Cinnamon Sedge Pupa	2	
	Grannom Wet Fly	8	
Adult Dry	Elk Hair Caddis	2, 8	6, 7, 8, or 10
	Fluttering Caddis	2	
	Kings River Caddis	2	
	Quill-Wing Caddis	2	
	Henryville Special	8	

(Note: See p. 28 for information on references and p. 32 for information on tactics.)

References

Caddisflies have recently received a lot of attention in the angling press. Two books, *Caddisflies* and *The Caddis and the Angler*, are listed here. Technical texts are also listed.

Harris, T.L. *Environmental Requirements and Pollution Tolerance of Trichoptera*. Cincinnati, Ohio: Environ. Monit. Sup. Lab., Off. Res. Dev. U.S.E.P.A., 1978.

LaFontaine, Gary. *Caddisflies*. New York: Nick Lyons Books, 1980.

Ross, H.H. *The Caddis Flies, or Trichoptera of Illinois*. Illinois: Bull. Ill. Nat. Hist. Surv. 23. 1944. (Reprint: 1972, Entomol. Rep. Specialists, Los Angeles.).

Solomon, Larry, and Eric Leiser. *The Caddis and the Angler*. Harrisburg, Pennsylvania: Stackpole Books, 1977.

Wiggins, Glen B. *Larvae of the North American Caddisfly Genera*. Toronto: University of Toronto Press, 1977.

11. True Flies: Order Diptera

Key to Diptera Larvae, p. 158
Key to Diptera Adults, p. 159

The order of true flies or Diptera contains a tremendous variety of species. The majority of species are terrestrial and are not important to fishermen as larvae. The adults of many terrestrial species, however, frequent the vegetation along the shores of lakes and rivers and often end up on the water's surface where fish feed on them.

Aquatic Diptera make up a small portion of the entire order, but there are still several thousand species that live underwater during part of their life cycle. The tremendous diversity of Diptera makes their identification difficult at best. Specialists often spend a lifetime trying to learn a single family. Obviously a fisherman must be content with a far more general approach if he or she is going to have any time left to fish.

Basic Identification and Similar Orders

While there are thousands of species, several dominant features make Diptera fairly easy to identify to order. Larvae lack jointed legs, giving their body the appearance of a segmented tube. Short, fleshy, unjointed legs called prolegs may be present on the thorax and/or abdomen, and the head of many species appears to be absent. Adults have only two wings, which gives the order its name: Di = two and Ptera = wing. The hind wings have been replaced by short peglike stalks called halteres. In flight they perform like small gyroscopes, keeping the insect on a straight course. Pupae often have wing pads and legs fused to the body, and only two wing pads will be present. Antennae are typically shorter than the body and are held tightly alongside the head. Larvae may occasionally be confused with aquatic beetle or moth larvae. Adults are most often confused with small mayflies or caddisflies. The following chart will help you distinguish between these groups.

Nymphs

Identifying Characters	Diptera	Beetles	Moths
Thoracic Legs (pairs)	0	3, a few species with none	3
Head	Variously shaped and developed; may or may not be visible	Well developed and visible	Well developed and visible
Prolegs	Often present on abdomen and/or thorax	None	Present on abdomen only

Adults

Identifying Characters	Diptera	Mayflies	Caddis flies
Wings	2	4, some species with only 2	4
Tails	0	2 or 3	0
Antennae	Short, no longer than length of head	Short, no longer than length of head	Long, body-length or longer

Size Range

With such a great variety of species, it's no surprise that Diptera have an extensive range of sizes. Larvae may range from 1mm to over 100mm long (1/16"-4"). This would equal hook sizes of #28 to #4 3XL. However, most Diptera important to fishermen are relatively small, ranging in length from 3-12mm (1/8"-1/2") and requiring hook sizes from #22 to #12. Pupae and adults are smaller than their corresponding larvae. Body lengths may range from 1-50mm (1/16"-2"). Hook sizes most commonly used are #22 to #12.

Life Cycle

All Diptera go through complete metamorphosis. The duration of each stage varies considerably between species. Many species produce more than one generation a year, and in warm waters some species may produce three, four, or even five generations a year.

Stage	Average Duration	Extremes
Egg	3-4 days	A few hours to several months
Larva	4-6 months	One week to 5-7 years
Pupa	5-10 days	1 or 2 days to 3 or 4 months
Adult	5-10 days	A few hours to 3 or 4 months

The wide variation in development time for Diptera makes it difficult to predict emergence dates. As water temperatures warm, each stage develops more rapidly. For example, during warm weather mosquitoes can complete one generation in about a week. In the Arctic, on the other hand, midges may take seven years to complete one generation.

Larval development typically takes several months. Most larvae molt three or four times during their development, but some black flies molt six or seven times. Diptera larvae show all types of feeding behavior. They may be predators, scavengers, filter feeders, or plant feeders. Most larvae are poor swimmers and live in bottom sediments or on rocks. Many species found in streams commonly drift in the current, where they are an important part of the diet of fish.

Pupae may develop underwater or on land, depending on the species. During development they're usually protected in a cocoon or in the covering of the last larval exoskeleton, called a puparium. Some pupae, such as mosquitoes, are active and exposed in open water. Once mature, most pupae swim or float to the water's surface for adult emergence. Pupae rising to the surface offer some of the best fishing opportunities, as fish find them easy meals.

Most adult Diptera will be found on the foliage along the banks of streams and rivers. This is where many species mate. Others mate in the air in large swarms, which are typically seen over the water on warm evenings. Depending on the species, eggs are laid on the water's surface, on the lake or stream bottom, or inside the stems of aquatic plants. Egg laying often provides the best time to imitate the adults, since they are readily available to fish during this time.

North American Distribution and Abundance
Aquatic Groups Only

Region	# of Families	# of Genera
East	26	318
Central	24	330
West	26	330
Total in N.A.	28	422

Approximate number of North American species: 5,000+ species with aquatic larval stages; 16,000+ species total

Habitat Preferences

There is probably no group of aquatic insects that has been able to exploit more habitats than the Diptera. Larvae are found in every imaginable type of habitat and are frequently the only aquatic insect present in extreme habitats such as hot springs and Arctic streams. The following chart shows how many families occur in different habitats.

Habitat Type	# of Families
Streams and rivers:	
Moderate to fast currents—	15
Slow currents—	17
Lakes and ponds:	
Near shore areas—	16
Deep water on bottom or in water—	5
Wet margins of lakes or streams:	17
Marine beaches and intertidal zones:	11
Salt marshes or estuaries:	9
Tree holes or plant cups:	8

It's obvious from this chart that Diptera will be found anywhere fish live and in many places they can't.

Identification

Because of the difficulty in identification of Diptera beyond the order level, the following keys divide the order into three groups: midges, crane flies, and other Diptera. Midges and crane flies are the most important groups of aquatic Diptera for flyfishers to learn to recognize. Other Diptera includes many types of flies that occasionally become abundant and important to imitate. Mosquitoes, black flies, horse flies, deer flies, marsh flies, and snipe flies are just a few examples.

Key to Diptera Larvae

This key will help you identify Diptera larvae to useful levels. Midges and crane flies will be separated from other Diptera, since they're of the most interest to flyfishermen.

1a. If head capsule is distinct and clearly visible, and first thoracic segment and last abdominal segment have a pair of ventral prolegs; and if body is evenly segmented without projections, gill filaments, or swellings and is generally small, less than 6mm (1/4"), with variable colors, it is a MIDGE. Go to p. 161.

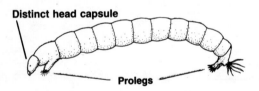

Distinct head capsule

Prolegs

1b. If the head capsule is not distinct, and characteristics vary from the midge's, go to **2**.

2a. If head capsule is well-developed but partially or fully retracted within first thoracic segment, making it difficult to observe, and last abdominal segment typically has two obvious spiracles (breathing holes) bordered by 1-6 finger-like lobes, it is a CRANE FLY. Go to p. 163.

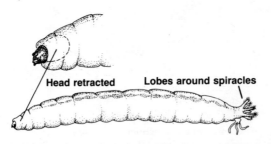

Head retracted   **Lobes around spiracles**

2b. If the head capsule is not retracted and other features show variation from those described above, it is one of the OTHER DIPTERA. Go to p. 164.

Key to Diptera Adults

Like the Key to Diptera Larvae, this key will separate the midges and crane flies from the other Diptera. This simplifies the key and makes it more useful to the fisherman.

1a. If antennae are longer than the thorax and composed of at least 6 segments, go to **2**.

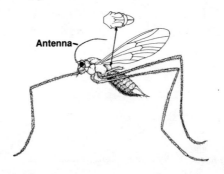

Antenna

1b. If antennae are composed of 5 or fewer segments and are shorter than the thorax, it is one of the OTHER DIPTERA. Go to p. 164.

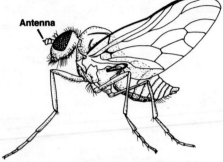

2a. If the mesonotum has a distinct V-shaped suture or impression, and legs are very long in relation to the body size; and if size ranges from 12-50mm (1/2"-2"), it is a CRANE FLY. Go to p. 163.

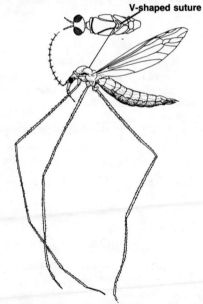

2b. If mesonotum lacks a V-shaped suture or impression, go to **3**.

3a. If postnotum is elongated with a median longitudinal groove or furrow, and body and wings are slender; and if mouth parts are reduced, non-biting, and the insect is generally small, from 1-10mm (1/32"-1/2"), it is a MIDGE. Go to p. 161.

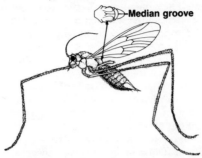

3b. If postnotum lacks median groove or furrow, and other characteristics vary from those listed above, it is one of the OTHER DIPTERA. Go to p. 164.

Midges

Major families and genera of midges:

Families	Genera (# of species)
Chironomidae	175+ genera (1,000+)

The term "midge" in common usage refers to any small insect. As used here, however, it applies only to members of the family Chironomidae. Even though this is only one family, there are more than 175 genera and 1,000 species of midges in North America alone. Few other families of aquatic insects present such great diversity.

The characteristics given in the preceding keys make recognition of midges fairly easy. But identification beyond the family level is a difficult, tedious task requiring special keys and techniques. Part of the problem is that all of the species look very similar. Only their size and color varies noticeably, and those are not reliable characteristics for identification, even though they are important for pattern selection.

Midges are important as food in all of their life stages— larva, pupa, and adult. Their importance in the ecology of streams and lakes, in fact, is often underestimated because of their small size. Juvenile fish, for example, depend heavily on midge larvae for food. Adult fish also feed heavily on these tiny morsels, often to the exclusion of larger and seemingly more obvious food. In streams, larvae consistently drift in the currents, increasing their availability to fish. Midge larvae also live in nearly every type of aquatic habitat, and what they lack in size, they make up for in numbers. This means that wherever fish live they will likely find significant quantities of midges to feed on.

Midge pupae develop on the bottom of streams or lakes, either covered by bottom debris or inside silken cocoons spun by the larvae. They mature quickly. After a few days to a week, they leave the safety of the bottom behind and swim with a slow wiggling motion to the surface. Fish often feed selectively on these rising pupae. During an emergence, pupae are the most important stage of midge to imitate. Fish patterns dead drift or with a very slow retrieve. You must experiment with fishing at different depths to produce the best results, since fish take the pupae anywhere from the bottom to the surface. This is particularly important in lakes.

Adult midges can also be important to imitate. They first become available to fish while they sit on the water's surface after escaping the pupal shuck. Later, mating or egg-laying swarms often form over the water. This provides fish a second opportunity to feed on the adults. Dead drifting small dry flies generally works best, but giving the fly subtle twitches can at times bring up a reluctant fish.

Midge hatches occur throughout the year. The midge's small size and the selective feeding by large fish that frequently occurs during a midge hatch demands all the skills of the flyfisher. The small, unglamorous midge offers one of the ultimate challenges of flyfishing... and one of the ultimate thrills.

Major Hatches of Midges

Name	Emergence	Size	Dist.
Midges	Year round	L:1-20mm	E C W
Chironomidae		P:1-15mm	
		A:1-15mm	

Major Patterns and Tactics for Midges

Stage	Patterns	Ref.	Tactics
Larva	Polly's Midge Larva	4	1, 8
Pupa	TDC	2, 3, 8	2, 8, or 10
	PKCK	3, 8	
Adult	Midge Dry	2, 5	6, 7, or 8
	Griffith's Gnat	2, 6	

(Note: See p. 28 for information on references and p. 32 for information on tactics.)

Crane Flies

Major families and genera of crane flies:

Families	Genera (# of species)
Tipulidae	*Tipula* (30)
	Dicranota (55)
	Hexatoma (34)
	Limnophila (40)

Crane flies form a second important group of aquatic Diptera. Not all crane flies have aquatic stages, however. The majority of species are terrestrial, and the larvae live in the soil. Aquatic crane flies are still quite diverse, with approximately 34 genera and over 1,000 species known in North America.

Crane fly larvae can be recognized by their tube-like body, and a head which is well developed but retracted inside the first thoracic segment, making it appear absent. Pulling back the cuticle of the first thoracic segment will expose the head. The rear of the abdomen on most species contains two large breathing holes, called spiracles. They appear as dark round spots and are often thought to be eyes. Larvae range in size from 10-100mm (3/8"-4").

Adult crane flies are mosquito-like in appearance but lack biting mouthparts. They are relatively large insects with very long legs. In flight their legs trail behind the body and often look like tails. As a result, it's easy to confuse them with flying mayflies at first glance.

Larva live in the bottom sediments of streams and lakes. They are found in all types of currents and bottom materials. While they can be quite abundant, most remain well hidden under gravel or debris and, therefore, are not readily available to fish. They are most important to imitate following a period of high water, which washes them out of the bottom.

Aquatic crane fly adults remain close to the water and frequently get caught in the surface tension. Females crawl on the sides of submerged rocks or plants to lay their eggs. This behavior is typically heaviest on warm summer afternoons. At such times, spider-type dry flies skated across the surface can be effective patterns.

Pupae develop on the margins of streams and lakes or above water in moist soil. Thus, they are not available to fish nor are they important to imitate.

Major Hatches of Crane Flies

Name	Emergence	Size	Dist.
Crane Fly	Apr-Sep	L:10-100mm	E C W
Tipulidae		P:5-25mm	
		A:5-25mm	

Major Patterns and Tactics for Crane Flies

Stage	Patterns	Ref.	Tactics
Larva	Giant Crane Fly Larva	7	1
Adult	Darbee Crane Fly	7	6, 7, or 8

(Note: See p. 28 for information on references and p. 32 for information on tactics.)

Other Diptera

This classification includes the wide variety of remaining aquatic flies. Terrestrial adult Diptera will also key to this group. Without further identification, it isn't possible to separate terrestrial adults from their aquatic cousins. Larvae and pupae collected from the water can be assumed to be aquatic forms.

The importance of this large group of flies varies widely. In general, they are important to imitate occasionally, most often in the summer. But when they are concentrated and abundant, fish will feed on them selectively.

The following list covers the major families found in this group along with their common names and general habitat in which they live.

Family	Common Name	Habitat
Culicidae	Mosquitoes	Still water
Ptychopteridae	Phantom Crane Flies	Still water
Blephariceridae	Net-Winged Midges	Running water
Chaoboridae	Phantom Midges	Still water
Ceratopogonidae	No-see-ums	Still and running water
Simuliidae	Black Flies	Running water
Tabanidae	Horse Flies and Deer Flies	Still and running water
Stratiomyidae	Soldier Flies	Still and running water
Athericidae	Snipe Flies	Running water
Empididae	Dance Flies	Running water

These Diptera obviously cover many sizes, colors, and shapes, and they are found in all types of aquatic habitats. Most larvae live in bottom sediments where their availability to fish is marginal. The pupae of most species develop out of the water in moist soil, where they are also unimportant to fish. Adults occasionally make useful models for imitation, when the naturals are concentrated near the water. At such times, a dry fly of appropriate size, color, and shape should be fished with an action similar to that of the natural.

References

Most texts dealing specifically with the aquatic Diptera are quite technical. The flyfisher will find the more general coverage in the following books to be most helpful.

McCafferty, W. Patrick. *Aquatic Entomology*. Boston: Science Books International, 1981.

Merritt, R.W., and K.W. Cummins. *An Introduction to the Aquatic Insects of North America*. Dubuque, Iowa: Kendall/Hunt Publishing Co., 1984 (2nd ed.).

Pennak, Robert W. *Fresh-Water Invertebrates of the United States*. New York: John Wiley & Sons, Inc., 1978 (2nd ed.).

12. Beetles: Order Coleoptera

Beetles form the largest insect order with over 300,000 known species in the world. While only about 5,000 of these species are aquatic, Coleoptera still represents one of the largest groups of aquatic insects.

The great variety of beetles, both terrestrial and aquatic, provides fish many feeding opportunities. Terrestrial adults, for example, often fall in the water and become food for fish. The number and diversity of aquatic species means that beetles will be present in nearly all types of aquatic habitats.

Even with the large variety and wide distribution of aquatic beetles, they tend to be of minor importance to fishermen. Many species live in habitats unsuitable for game fish. Others live in tangles of debris where they are not readily available to fish. And in general, the numbers of aquatic beetles never seem to reach those of other aquatic insects, such as mayflies, stoneflies, or caddisflies. As a result, it's only important for the flyfisher to recognize when beetles are abundant and available to fish and to imitate them at those times.

The identification of beetles presents another problem. Their diversity complicates the process, but because most beetles can be imitated with a limited number patterns and tactics, identification of specific types is less important than for most other groups. **Therefore, this chapter does not present any keys to identify beetles beyond order.** The information presented applies to aquatic beetles in general and will provide you with the necessary information to imitate and fish them effectively.

Basic Identification and Similar Orders

The characteristics described in the keys to orders separates aquatic beetles from other aquatic insects. Beetle larvae present the greatest difficulties in identification and the greatest possible confusion with other groups. Except for a few species, beetle larvae all have three pair of jointed thoracic legs. The mouthparts are of the chewing type, although the mandibles of some species are hollow and adapted for sucking.

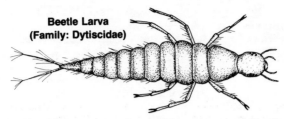

**Beetle Larva
(Family: Dytiscidae)**

Larvae breathe in a number of ways. Some have filamentous gills on the abdomen for obtaining dissolved oxygen from the water. Others have a breathing tube at the end of their abdomen that is periodically lifted above the water to breath surface air. Perhaps most unusual are those larvae that get their oxygen from the stems of underwater plants. Beetle larvae are most often confused with caddisflies, alderflies, and hellgrammites.

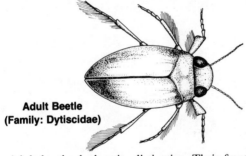

**Adult Beetle
(Family: Dytiscidae)**

Adult beetles look quite distinctive. Their front wings (called elytra) are hard and form a shell-like covering over the hind wings and abdomen. Only aquatic bugs (Hemiptera) have a similar appearance.

Larvae

Identifying Characters	Beetles	Alderflies	Hellgrammites	Caddisflies
Anal Hooks	0	0	4	2
Antennae	½ to as long as head	As long as head	As long as head	Minute
Gills	Various shapes and sizes or absent	Lateral abdominal filaments	Lateral abdominal filaments	Abdominal filaments present or absent

Adults

Identifying Characters	Beetles	Aquatic Hemiptera
Front Wings	Completely hardened forming a shell-like covering over hind wings and abdomen	Basal two thirds thick and leathery, apical portion membranous; form cover over hind wings and abdomen
Mouthparts	Chewing type	Piercing/sucking, needle-like in appearance
Antennae	Generally short (less than length of head) and often concealed under head	Short and concealed under head, or up to ½ body length

Size Range

Beetles as a whole show a greater range in sizes than any other order of insects; both the smallest and largest known insects are beetles. Aquatic beetles also come in a wide range of sizes. Mature larvae may range from 2-70mm (1/8"-2 3/4") and require hooks from #22 to #4 3XL to imitate them. Most larvae range from 10-25mm (3/8"-1") and can be imitated with hooks from #14 to #8 3XL. Adults range from 1-40mm (1/16"-1 5/8"). Hooks from #16 to #10 will imitate most adults.

Life Cycle

Beetles go through complete metamorphosis. The diversity of species results in a great variety in life cycles. Most species complete one generation per year, but others may take two to three years to complete one life cycle.

Stage	Average Duration	Extremes
Egg	1-3 weeks	3-4 months
Larva	6-8 months	1 month to 2-3 years
Pupa	2-3 weeks	2-3 months
Adult	2-3 months	1 week to 2-3 years

Most species lay their eggs in the spring. The larvae then develop through the summer. Pupation occurs in the fall with the adults then overwintering and mating and laying eggs the following spring. Some species overwinter as larvae or pupae and, occasionally, as eggs.

The larval stage is normally the longest. Many beetle larvae are fierce predators, while others feed on plants or detritus. Rotting wood is also a common food for numerous species. The predacious species are generally the most active and, therefore, the most available to fish. When mature, most larvae crawl out of the water to pupate.

Pupae develop under damp soil in a cell-like chamber dug by the larvae. Others spin submerged silk cocoons which contain bubbles of air for the pupa to breath. Most pupae mature in a few weeks.

The adult stage is usually the most active stage and typically lasts for several months. Many use their hind legs as oars and are good swimmers. Mating occurs in the water or on land. Adults also fly well, and after mating many disperse to other areas before laying their eggs. Eggs are typically laid on bottom substrates, on the leaves of aquatic plants, and occasionally in the stems of aquatic plants.

North American Distribution and Abundance

Region	# of Families	# of Genera
East	13	108
Central	12	95
West	16	117
Total in N.A.	16	174

Approximate number of North American species: 1,000 aquatic species; 30,000 species total

Habitat Preferences

Most species of aquatic beetles live in the water as larvae and adults. However, there are variations. In some species, only the larval stage is aquatic. More unusual are the species that have a terrestrial larval stage and an aquatic adult stage.

Aquatic beetles live in most freshwater habitats. Some, such as water pennies (Family: Psephenidae) and riffle beetles (Family: Elmidae), commonly occur in the fast riffle areas of streams and rivers. The greatest abundance and diversity of beetles, however, occur in slow-moving or still waters. In these habitats, two families stand out as most common and abundant—the predacious diving beetles (Family: Dytiscidae) and the water scavenger beetles (Family: Hydrophilidae).

Predacious diving beetles are fierce predators as both larvae and adults. Larvae are often called "water tigers" because of their hunting behavior. Adults swim with strong strokes of their oar-like hind legs. Water scavenger beetles are mainly predacious as larvae, but the adults feed on detritus and plant material.

Larvae and adults exhibit various behaviors. Most larvae are crawlers or climbers and do not swim. They spend most of their time on aquatic plants, tangles of wood debris, or detritus. Most adult beetles, on the other hand, are swimmers. As swimmers they spend more time in open water and are therefore more available to fish. Many larvae and most adults also rely on surface air for their oxygen. Thus, they must swim or crawl to the surface periodically. Larvae typically have a breathing tube which they project above the surface. Adults normally capture a bubble of air which they take underwater with them. These bubbles shine like glass beads.

Because the greatest abundance of aquatic beetles occurs in lakes and slow rivers, this is where they are most important to fishermen. As they crawl along the bottom searching for prey, the larvae are taken regularly by fish. Fish also find adults easy prey as the beetles swim back to the surface to replenish their air bubbles. Because both larvae and adults are aquatic, there isn't an emergence in the normal sense, although adults become more prevalent in the late summer, fall, and winter months. The following table lists the major families of beetles which are important to fishermen.

Major Families of Aquatic Beetles

Family	Common Name	Size	Dist.
Dytiscidae	Predacious Diving Beetles	L: 2-70mm A: 1-40mm	E C W
Hydrophilidae	Water Scavenger Beetles	L: 4-60mm A: 1-40mm	E C W
Amphizoidae	Trout-stream Beetles	L: 15-20mm A: 11-16mm	W
Gyrinidae	Whirligig Beetles	L: 5-30mm A: 3-15mm	E C W
Chrysomelidae	Leaf Beetles	L: 8-20mm A: 5-10mm	E C W

Major Patterns and Tactics for Aquatic Beetles

Stage	Patterns	Ref.	Tactis
Larva	Wooly Worm	2, 8	2, 3, 9, or 10
Adult	Water Boatman (color to match natural)	2, 6, 8	3 or 9

(Note: See p. 28 for information on references and p. 32 for information on tactics.)

References

Most texts dealing specifically with the aquatic beetles are quite technical. The flyfisher will find the more general coverage in the following books to be the most helpful.

McCafferty, W. Patrick. *Aquatic Entomology.* Boston: Science Books International, 1981.

Merritt, R.W. and K.W. Cummins. *An Introduction to the Aquatic Insects of North America.* Dubuque, Iowa: Kendall/Hunt Publishing Co., 1984 (2nd ed.).

Pennak, Robert W. *Fresh-Water Invertebrates of the United States.* New York: John Wiley & Sons, Inc., 1978 (2nd ed.).

13. Aquatic Moths: Order Lepidoptera

The order Lepidoptera, which includes moths and butterflies, is certainly one of the best known groups of terrestrial insects. Who hasn't chased a butterfly across an open field? And old butterfly collections from past school days are common relics often lost to attics and closets. Even with the popular interest in butterflies, most people are unaware that there are a number of species of Lepidoptera that are aquatic as larvae and pupae.

Granted, with over 10,000 species of Lepidoptera in North America, the approximately 50 known aquatic species make up a very small portion of the order. Another 100 species are considered semiaquatic and live in close association with aquatic habitats. Nearly all truly aquatic Lepidoptera belong to the family Pyralidae, which contains numerous terrestrial species as well.

Aquatic moths are of minor importance to fishermen most of the time. While they occur across the country, their populations tend to be widely dispersed. When they are found in large numbers, however, they can become concentrated enough to produce selective feeding by fish.

Because of the sparse fauna and relatively minor importance of aquatic Lepidoptera to fishermen, it is rarely necessary to identify specimens past the order level. **Therefore, this chapter presents no keys for further identification.** The information presented concerning aquatic Lepidoptera will apply to nearly all species and situations of interest to the flyfisher.

Basic Identification and Similar Orders

Aquatic larvae have the same basic characteristics as their terrestrial counterparts. Most definitive of these traits is the presence of short, unsegmented legs (prolegs) on abdominal segments 3, 4, 5, 6, and 10. These prolegs are tipped with fine hooks called crochets (seen with a hand lens or microscope). Some aquatic species also have filamentous gill tufts on the abdominal segments. Other aquatic larvae that could be confused with aquatic moths include beetle, Diptera, and caddisfly larvae.

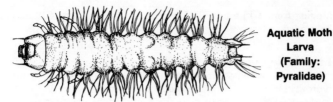

**Aquatic Moth
Larva
(Family:
Pyralidae)**

Aquatic moth adults are terrestrial, except for one species where the female remains underwater. In appearance they look like one of the many small, common, drab-colored moths. Unless they're observed emerging from the water or laying eggs there, it can be difficult separating them from terrestrial forms. Adult moths most closely resemble caddisfly adults.

Larvae			
Identifying Characters	**Aquatic Moths**	**Beetles**	**Caddis- flies**	**Diptera**
Thoracic Legs (pairs)	3	3, rarely	3	0
Abdominal Prolegs	Present	Absent	Absent	Present
Prolegs have crochets	Yes	N/A	N/A	No
Anal Hooks	None	None	2	None

Adults		
Identifying Characters	**Aquatic Moths**	**Caddisflies**
Wings	4, of similar size, held flat over abdomen and covered with flat, scale-like hairs	4, of similar size, held tent-shaped over abdomen and covered with fine hairs
Antennae	Shorter than body	Body length or longer
Mouthparts	Long tube-like siphon coiled under the head when not in use	Reduced, without tube-like siphon

Size Range

Most aquatic moths are small to moderate in size. Mature larvae range from 3-30mm (1/8"-1 1/4"). Hook sizes from #18 to #10 will cover most species. Adults are smaller than the larvae, ranging from 3-15mm (1/8"-5/8"). Hooks from #18 to #12 may be needed.

Life Cycle

All Lepidoptera go through complete metamorphosis. There are typically one or two generations of aquatic moths a year. Available food and water temperature are the major factors determining the time required to complete a life cycle.

Stage	Average Duration	Extremes
Egg	1-3 weeks	1 month or more
Larva	7-9 months	3-4 months
Pupa	2-4 weeks	1 week to more than a month
Adult	1-3 weeks	1 day to 2 months

The life cycle of aquatic moths is very similar to that of caddisflies. The aquatic moth's larval stage is the longest lived and the stage that typically passes through the winter. Aquatic larvae feed on algae covering rocks or on leaves or stems of aquatic plants. During the summer when water temperatures warm, larvae grow quickly. Two and sometimes three generations a year are possible in warm climates.

Typical Moth Pupa

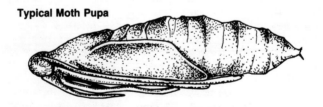

Pupae develop underwater inside silken cocoons. At emergence, the adults cuts out of the cocoon and swims or floats to the surface. This is perhaps the most vulnerable part of the life cycle and is the best stage to imitate. After mating, females crawl down the sides of rocks or dive into the water and swim to the bottom to lay their eggs. These adults are also available to fish, but egg laying normally occurs at night, reducing the opportunities to imitate them.

North American Distribution and Abundance

Region	# of Families	# of Genera
East	1	11
Central	1	7
West	1	9
Total in N.A.	1	16

Approximate number of North American species: 50 aquatic species; 10,000 species total

Habitat Preferences

Aquatic larvae are found in a variety of habitats. Several species select rocky bottoms in the swift currents of mountain streams. They live on the surface of the rocks where they scrape off the thin layer of algae called periphyton. For protection from the current, the larvae cover themselves with a thick blanket of silk which is firmly attached to the rock. The larvae feed within the safety of this silk housing.

Most species, however, live in slow-moving or still water where aquatic plants are abundant. These larvae feed on the leaves and stems of the plants. Most roam freely as they feed. A few feed under silk webs, while others bore inside plant tissues to feed. Larvae are not readily available to fish in most cases because of their blanket covering and feeding behavior.

Pupae of most aquatic species develop underwater inside cocoons spun by the larvae. In streams, these cocoons are built under the silk blankets. In lakes, cocoons are attached to the stems or leaves of aquatic plants. Once mature, pupae do not leave the cocoon and swim to the surface as caddis pupae do. Instead, the change from pupa to adult takes place within the cocoon. The adult then swims to the surface.

Adults normally emerge at night. They are not strong swimmers and often struggle for several minutes to reach the surface. Once on the surface, their wings may take 30 minutes to dry completely. Adults spend most of their time on foliage near the banks. After mating there they return to the water at night to lay their eggs.

The adult stage is by far the most available one to fish. Adult moths are rarely seen by fishermen, however, because of their nocturnal behavior. In streams or lakes where large populations are present, night fishing or fishing at dawn and dusk with adult imitations retrieved under the surface will provide you with the best opportunities to catch fish that are feeding on aquatic moths.

Major Hatches of Aquatic Moths

Name	Emergence	Size	Dist.
Aquatic Moths	May-Sep	L: 3-35mm	E C W
Pyralidae		P: 3-15mm	
		A: 3-15mm	

Major Patterns and Tactics for Aquatic Moths

Stage	Patterns	Ref.	Tactics
Larva	Cream Caddis Worm	8	1 or 2
Adult	White or Gray Miller Wet Fly	8	2, 3, or 5

References

Most texts dealing specifically with the aquatic Lepidoptera are quite technical. The flyfisher will find the more general coverage in the following books to be the most helpful.

McCafferty, W. Patrick. *Aquatic Entomology*. Boston: Science Books International, 1981.

Merritt, R.W. and K.W. Cummins. *An Introduction to the Aquatic Insects of North America*. Dubuque, Iowa: Kendall/Hunt Publishing Co., 1984 (2nd ed.).

Pennak, Robert W. *Fresh-Water Invertebrates of the United States*. New York: John Wiley & Sons, Inc., 1978 (2nd ed.).

Glossary

The definitions here provide a quick reference for use during the identification process. For more information on the terms and their applications, check the sections on insect anatomy in Chapter 1 and read the introductory material in the chapters in which you find the terms.

cercus (pl. cerci): A typically slender filamentous appendage on the tenth abdominal segment; commonly called the tail.

cubital intercalaries: Typically paired, unconnected longitudinal veins occuring in the insect wing between the cubitus and anal veins.

dorsal: Of or belonging to the upper surface.

dun: In mayflies, the first winged stage, technically called the subimago. The dun is not yet a true adult since it cannot reproduce in this stage.

exoskeleton: The outside covering or skeleton of insects.

halteres: The modified, stalk-like hind wings of adult Diptera.

instar: The period or stage between molts during nymph or larva development.

labial palp (pl. palpi): Segmented, finger-like structure of varying length found on the side of the labium.

labium: The lower lip, the structure that typically forms the floor of the mouth.

labrum: The uppermost part of the mouth; the upper lip. It covers the base of the mandibles and forms the roof of the mouth.

larva (pl. larvae): The immature stage or stage between the egg and pupa, in insects that go through complete metamorphosis.

lateral filaments: Filamentous structures (often gills) projecting from the sides of body segments.

mandibles: The first pair of jaws. They may be stout and tooth-like in insects with chewing mouthparts or needle-shaped in insects with sucking mouthparts.

maxilla (pl. maxillae): The second pair of jaws. Often modified in shape depending on the type of feeding.

maxillary palp (pl. palpi): Segmented finger-like structure on the side of the maxilla, typically sensory in function.

mesonotum: The upper surface of the second thoracic segment.

mesothorax: Second or middle segment of the thorax.

metamorphosis: The series of changes an insect passes through during its development from egg to adult.

metathorax: Third segment of the thorax (closest to the abdomen).

molting: The process where the old exoskeleton is shed and a new, slightly larger one forms. This process occurs during the growth of immature insects.

morphology: An animal's form or structure.

notum (pl. nota): The dorsal or upper part of a segment.

nymph: The young or immature stage of insects that go through incomplete metamorphosis.

ocellus (pl. ocelli): The simple eye of nymph or adult insects, consisting of a single bead-like lens. May occur singly or in small groups.

ovipositing: The act of laying eggs.

pleuron (pl. pleura): The lateral region of any segment of the insect body; typically refers to the lateral region of the thorax.

postnotum: A plate on the upper surface of the thorax occuring between two of the thoracic segments.

prolegs: Unjointed, fleshy appendages that serve as legs.

prothorax: First segment of the thorax (closest to the head).

pupa (pl. pupae): The intermediate stage between the larva and adult in insects that go through complete metamorphosis.

shuck: The old empty exoskeleton left behind after molting occurs.

spinner: In mayflies, the second and final winged stage, technically called the imago. The spinner is the true adult stage of mayflies.

spinner falls: The process of adult mayflies falling on the water to lay their eggs after mating is completed.

stemmata: The simple eye spots found on the larval stage of insects that go through complete metamorphosis.

sternum (pl. sterna): The ventral or lower portion of any segment, or often specifically, the underside of an insect's thorax.

tarsus (pl. tarsi): The foot; the jointed appendage attached at the apex of the tibia.

tergum (pl. terga): The dorsal or upper portion of any body segment.

thorax: One of the three major body sections of insects, occuring between the head and abdomen.

ventral: Of or belonging to the lower surface.

wing pads: The pouch-like structure found on nymphs and pupae that hold the developing wings of the adult.

wing venation: The pattern of veins which run through and provide support for insect wings. The pattern of veins is distinct within specific insect groups and is often used in identificaiton.

Index